Realm of the
Wise One

KEVINHUNTER

WARRIOR
OF LIGHT
PRESS
Los Angeles, California

Warrior Of Light Press
www.kevin-hunter.com

Body, Mind & Spirit/Spiritualism
Inspiration & Personal Growth

PRODUCTION CREDITS:
Project Editor: James Szopo

Acknowledgements

Thank you to my spiritual posse that consists of God, my personal sports team of Angels, Guides, Archangels and Saints. Thank you also to my Editor, James Szopo, who is a Star Person that has described me as being a little rough around the edges. This is a truthful statement about the personality of a Wise One.

Chapters

Author's Note

All *Warrior of Light* books are infused with practical messages and guidance that my Spirit team has taught and shared with me revolving around many different topics. The main goal is to fine tune your body, mind and soul. This improves humanity one person at a time. You are a Divine communicator and perfectly adjusted and capable of receiving messages from Heaven. This is for your benefit in order to live a happier, richer life. It is your individual responsibility to respect yourself and this planet while on your journey here.

The messages and information enclosed in this and all of the *Warrior of Light* books may be in my own words, but they do not come from me. They come from God, the Holy Spirit, my Spirit team of guides, angels and sometimes certain Archangels and Saints. I am merely the liaison or messenger in delivering and interpreting the intentions of what they wish to communicate. They love that I talk about them and share this stuff as it gets other people to work with them too!

There is one main hierarchy Saint who works with me leading the pack. His name is Nathaniel. He is often brutally truthful and forceful, as he does not mince words. There may be topics in this and my other books that might bother you or make you uncomfortable. He asks that you examine the underlying cause of this discomfort and come to terms with the fear attached. He cuts right to the heart of humanity without apology. I have learned quite a bit from him while adopting his ideology, which is Heaven's philosophy as a whole.

I am one with the Holy Spirit and have many Spirit Guides and Angels around me. As my connections to the other side grew to be daily over the course of my life, more of them joined in behind the others. I have often seen, sensed, heard and been privy to the dozens of magnificent lights that crowd around me on occasion.

If I use the word "He" when pertaining to God, this does not mean that I am advocating that he is a male. Simply replace the word, "He" with one you are comfortable using to identify God for you to be. This goes for any gender I use as examples. When I say, "spirit team", I am referring to a team of 'Guides and Angels'. The purpose of the *Warrior of Light* books is to empower and help you improve yourself, your life and humanity as a whole. It does not matter if you are a beginner or well versed in the subject matter. There may be something that reminds you of something you already know or something that you were unaware of. We all have much to share with one another, as we are all one in the end. This book and all of the *Warrior of Light* series of books contain information and directions on how to reach the place where you can be a fine tuned instrument to receive your own messages from your own Spirit team.

Some of my personal stories are infused and sprinkled in the books. This is in order for you to see how it works effectively for me. With some of my methods, I hope that you gain insight, knowledge or inspiration. It may prompt you to recall incidents where you were receiving heavenly messages in your own life. There are helpful ways that you can improve your existence and have a connection with Heaven throughout this book. Doing so will greatly transform yourself in all ways allowing you to attract wonderful circumstances at higher levels and live a happier more content life.

~ Kevin Hunter

Preface

CHANNELING

One warm afternoon in the Summer, I spent a couple of hours on the beach channeling messages from the other side. This was material coming through my crown chakra that would later become the book you hold in your hand. Standing at the foot of the ocean with my phone, I frantically typed the messages coming in using my right thumb. This is one useful tool that technology provides and that is when using it to positively benefit others. The Wise One perfectionist in me would scroll back into the notepad on the phone and start correcting and editing words here and there. Luke, my main Spirit Guide shouted, "Edit later! We're not done!" I grumbled, shook it off, and stopped my perfectionist ways....temporarily anyway.

Channeling beyond fifteen minutes is already quite a bit! I was wishing I had my computer as there was an abundant amount of information sifting into me all at once and without warning. This isn't surprising considering that I was hanging out in nature next to the detoxing ocean. Nature is where the messages from Heaven come in clearer. The ocean has the power to immediately lift off every stress cell that might exist within and around you. Take big healthy breathes in when you head into nature.

Every time I was getting ready to leave the beach, my Spirit team would feed me more information. I knew if I left prematurely that by the time I got home and settled in again to continue channeling, then the messages would be gone. Moving into an altered state of consciousness in a channel is ever shifting. By the time I would get home, who knows what state I'd be in to receive messages. I must've thrown my phone into my bag a dozen times as I prepped to leave. I'd start climbing the huge boulder rocks that sit in front of a small strip of sand that sits in front of the Pacific Ocean. My trek up the rocks would begin as quickly as it ended. My Spirit team would speak more words into my clairaudience channel. I'd say, "Ugh, hang on. Shoooot." I'd climb back down again with great speed. Quickly yanking the phone out of my bag I began typing again in this stream of consciousness. I usually have a little notepad with me, but on this particular day I discovered that I forgot to bring it.

After doing this procedure of attempting to leave the beach a couple of times, I learned my lesson to not go anywhere. Just sit tight and relax for awhile. Instead, I paced back and forth around the same spot in front of the ocean like a panther. I'm holding my phone with one hand and mumbling my team's words and images as I typed as fast as I could. To those few people that passed by, I must've looked mad and insane. I certainly won't stop when I'm in the zone. Luckily, they didn't seem to flinch or be bothered, but were more curious and drawn in. They hung around me for awhile and remained quiet as they absorbed the warmth of the energy light that had risen and grown around me.

Channeling is an odd combination of using energy that drains while uplifting and overwhelms at the same time. This process sometimes takes months to fall into the right frequency. To go back home and be on my Spirit teams frequency while merging beautifully with them is always uplifting and fun, but takes a little work to get there and be in it. Then when I come back from that space, I more or less collapse wherever I happen to be. I have to bring my energy levels back up again. It's a strange euphoric kind of feeling.

Realm of the

Wise One

Introduction

In the Spirit World, there are nearly a dozen dimensions. These dimensions house different families of spirits. The families might consist of angels, spirit guides, deceased loved ones, saints, ascended masters or archangels. There are also various spirits in different forms who come from a variety of different "Realms" that exist on the other side. In this book, "Realm of the Wise One", I discuss the Wise Ones on the other side as well as those who have incarnated into a human body. This is a realm I know quite a bit about since I have incarnated from the Realm of the Wise One. It's always fun to go back home. This book is for all Wise Ones and those who personally know a Wise One. It is also for anyone looking to gain additional knowledge surrounding behavior patterns and purposes of some of the souls that surround you as Wise Ones.

My Spirit team has shared with me where I come from on numerous occasions throughout the course of my human life. They've shown me what my home is like, where I come from, who I really am in truth beyond this life, and a glimpse of my soul back home where I reside. Other Wise Ones and those from some of the various Realms may sense familiarity, while others might fall into skepticism. This book requires some suspension of disbelief for those hardened, jaded

1

and practical human souls who are not used to being connected with the other side. We are travelling into the Spirit World or what some call Heaven. Therefore you will know that it is nothing like the density ticking time bomb of planet Earth.

In the first chapter of this book, I take you to the Spirit World where the Wise Ones reside. I describe the visuals of what it's like. It is also the longest chapter in this book, so you'll need to exercise patience while keeping an open mind. It may feel much like a cartoon or something from a movie not yet made. In the second and third chapter, we dive into why those from a Realm incarnate on Earth as well as some of the core Realms. From Chapter Four through the rest of the book, we will discuss in great length all things Wise Ones in human form. We'll cover an abundant amount of information surrounding their personalities, behavior patterns, purposes and much more. It is important to first start off by describing who the Wise Ones are and where they come from in the next dimension, before moving into the Wise Ones around you on Earth. You may even be a Wise One yourself! There are books on the market that feature chapters or information surrounding the Wise One, but this is one of the first books devoted solely to the Realm of the Wise Ones.

Travel with me now to the magical world of the Wise Ones. Remember to keep an open mind and heart in learning how to recognize those human souls around you who are indeed from the Realm of the Wise One.

Chapter One

The Wise Ones in the Spirit World

A massive waterfall sound gushes like an exploded geyser filling up my *clairaudience* channel. It overtakes any other sound that exists around me in real time. It overflows my heart and I am transported home again. The waterfall is not a quiet brook trickling lightly as if in a peaceful Zen Garden. The sound is massive as if you are standing in front of Niagara Falls. This waterfall spills over a jagged rock formation. There are several other waterfalls near it as they all fall freely with force and into the crystal clear blue water below. This water is not dark and has no pollution in it. It's so clean you can drink from it if you wanted to. The waterfall is loud enough that it's impossible not to be aware of the powerful presence it conveys. At the bottom of each of the waterfalls, steam rises upwards right back into the falling water enveloping it like a hug. At the top of the waterfall, there is a glimpse of a stone like structure protruding out with a bit of glow around it.

A sparkling ray of colored light shoots passed slightly above the top of the waterfall at great speed. If you blink you almost miss it when it stops and evaporates. There are sparkling lights in the distance soaring in different directions across the brightly lit skies. The weather is sunny and warm at a comfortable 75 degrees. There are exotic birds of every variety flying around and singing beautiful, heavenly sounds. The flowers are astoundingly vibrant, lush and emitting rich color. If you look close enough there are sparkles of light shining within and around each flower. They are alive much like the flowers that sing in the animated feature, *Alice in Wonderland*. There are fireflies, dragonflies and butterfly's travelling in packs to their homes in the nearby forest. They also have a spark of light that resembles the firework sparklers you see on the Fourth of July. You can hear and feel the electricity that surrounds them. The place is magically active with pulsating color. Flickers of light are painted everywhere like glitter run amass on a canvas painted by Jackson Pollock.

A darker violet ray of light moves about at the top of the waterfall. It soars down quickly landing on one of the large boulder rocks at the top of the waterfall. Fading out of the surrounding violet light, it appears to be a person draped in a long dark cloak and hood covering its face. There's a snapping sound and the cloak flies off to the side in mid-air almost like a magician with a cape. This cape evaporates into a million little lights and fades into the running water at the top of the cliff where the waterfall pours down. Looking closer at the figure, I see that it's me. I'm standing at the top of one of the waterfalls where the ray of light had evaporated. It looks like me, but not quite. It's not what

I'm familiar with when I look in the mirror at my human body on Earth. This is me not long before I agreed to incarnate into another Earthly life. I'm visibly strong with lean muscle and skin that glistens and shines. In fact, there is a slight enchanting glow of light around me that is uplifting just by being in that presence. There is a bow and arrow strapped to my back, yet there doesn't appear to be a strap or anything keeping it there. Whenever I move and jump from one spot to the next, the bow and arrow moves with me floating in the air behind my back. I look about twenty-five to thirty years old, young in human years, yet my soul is four hundred and seventy years old. I have incarnated on Earth frequently by choice. Many Wise Ones have incarnated on Earth numerous times over the course of human history for a specific purpose. Although the Earth's atmosphere has troubled many of them to the point where they've flown their hands in the air and cut out of here quickly.

There are animals living in this all natural habitat that is not destroyed by human souls. This habitat is a colorful theme park of gorgeous nature settings in all directions. Beyond the falling waterfalls sprouts a lush forest. Every blade of grass and tree brightly sparkles with varying shades of green color. Within that color are twinkling white light diamond stars. The forests here are perfectly safe for anyone without the fear of being attacked by man or a wild animal. The animals here do not harm anyone or anything. They have no need to since survival is not necessary. Everything needed is provided naturally. To a human mind this would seem much like fable magic. Magic energy is a big part of the Wise Ones nature. They manifest easily and effortlessly typically with their thoughts. They've built these wonders in the Spirit World by banding together and creating a world of paradise in the process.

Outside of the forest is a vast blue uncontaminated ocean. Its grandness is spread out like a blanket opened wide into oblivion. The Realms in the Spirit World or anywhere in Heaven for that matter are much like those tropical gorgeous photos of the islands and white sands you see in places like Hawaii, the Pacific or the Caribbean. The only difference is this is a hundred times more magnificent than a human soul can comprehend. Every sense is awakened and alive. This is from the visual, the hearing, the knowing and the feeling. All of your *clair* channels are working at 100% optimum levels without effort. It's not like on Earth, where human souls have to work hard through the density, heaviness and negative energy of the planet and their surroundings in order to be in tune if only for a little bit. Even on a human soul's best day, their *clair* channels are nothing like they are when in the Spirit World. It's like cranking your stereo up to full capacity. You can hide no secrets from one another with your thoughts, because on the other side, the communication is telepathic. Since your *clair* channels are off the charts on the other side, then you can imagine how nothing is hidden in the Spirit World. This doesn't mean that no one opens their mouths, and nor are they more perfect and powerful than anyone else. On the contrary, a great many conversations through talking happens, but isn't necessary if they don't want to.

Heaven is a word that is often equated to be blissful paradise. The word has many contexts such as when someone says, "When you die and go to Heaven". Some immediately equate it to a place of judgment, while others may use it when describing something pleasurable. "Oh, this is Heaven!" Human souls are less offended or jarred for some reason when the latter is said in that context. The ego in man loves to instill lower energy vibrations like fear, worry, anger, hate, punishment and guilt. Heaven is all beauty, all love, all joy and all knowingness. It's the counter opposite of what human souls like to preach or display in their daily behavior.

Many human souls dream of living an abundant happy life in a beautiful home that sits in paradise on Earth with a love companion. Yet on Earth this seems difficult to obtain for many of them, while in Heaven you have it the second you think of it. This is much like painting what you want onto a canvas. Those in the Wise One realm live in these tropical surroundings. They live in castle like homes and huts that sit in front of or in these beautiful natural wonders. It is quite interesting the way they build these homes. Some of these homes sit by the sea and others sit in magnificent gardens and forests. They love being out in nature and they often meditate on the different phases of the several moons that move about in their skies.

There is a Wise One standing outside one of the homes by the ocean in the Spirit world. She puts both her hands out about waste high and a shining white gate appears underneath her hands. She's not physically holding it, but it's an inch or two under her hand. She lets it go and the gate straps itself naturally into the sand. There is endless space that is manipulated by the power of the mind of the Spirits. No one lives near or on top of each other the way human souls do when they build home dwellings on Earth.

The creator of Superman, both the writer and artist came from what is called the Star Person realm. They received their creative idea by remembering where they came from and how easy it is to manipulate energy. As human souls, they likely were unaware of that, and would probably believe it to be a fragment of their imagination...or was it? Science Fiction comes from ideas and visions that are familiar in one's subconscious for that particular human soul.

This ocean that the female appearing Wise One home faces is no ordinary sea. It's free of pollution and glimmers like transparent glass. It's clear enough that you can see out into the distance for miles. In this ocean, reside fish of all types swimming around just like on Earth. Except these are not the dangerous predators that move about on Earth. The critters on Earth are often dangerous because they have a physical Earthly need to survive. In the Spirit World, there are sharks, but they are harmless. They are all spirit fish that morph in and out of light and physical forms.

There are dolphins and even merman, mermaids, Merfolk or Merpeople leaping with joy and grace in and out of the water. The Wise Ones often meet with the Merfolk at the foot of the sea. Since they can all morph into whatever they like, the Merfolk appear at the doorsteps of the Wise Ones homes by this sea. Just like popular mythology, their tails morph into legs when out of the water. Some discuss the work they're doing on Earth and the human soul they are guiding in order to accomplish this. Merfolk often ask the Wise Ones for guidance on the causes they're working on for Earth and other planets in other galaxies. This is not uncommon as the Wise One name is given this name because of who and what they are. They are all knowing. This sense of knowingness is connected to their *claircognizance* channel which is located through the crown chakra at the top of your soul. Wise Ones have lived so many lives before and come with an abundance of knowledge. Some of them on the other side join in with a departed soul during their transition back home.

Wise Ones in the spirit world and on earth are practical with an analytical mind. Many of the great Wise Ones in history have an equal balance of the emotional and rationale within them. It is split right down the middle. When those in a particular Realm need guidance on how to proceed with an action, or a troubled human soul they're working with, they often travel to the Realm where the Wise Ones exist or they telepathically communicate with one of choice or any. The Wise Ones received their name because they have been responsible for many of the positive changes made on Earth. They worked with the Star People to create the wonders in technology. Granted they knew that this would cause issues by cranking up the noise of the worlds that use it. On the flip side, they knew that this was what was going to also bring positive changes that are desperately needed. They knew things would get worse before they would get better. Unlike some circles on Earth and human life, in the Spirit World everyone works together when needed and without attitude.

Because the Wise Ones also reside in the heavenly mountains, deserts and forests, they mix and mingle with all those that live in those areas too. The Realm of the Wise Ones interconnects with the Realm of the Elementals in the forests. The Elementals include fairies, leprechauns, elves, gnomes, unicorns and other critters that a human soul would believe to be mythology or fiction. Just because you haven't seen or experienced something with your own eyes does not mean it's not true. In the Elemental realm are also those that reside in the water such as the MerFolk, Whales, Sharks and Dolphins. All of those in these Realms often choose to incarnate on Earth throughout its history in order to enact a specific change or changes. Since most human souls do not listen to their Spirit team of Guides and Angels, those residing in the Realms incarnate into a human body to apply their expertise into a situation that can help grow and prosper peace and joy on planet Earth. They know when they incarnate into a human body that it will not be easy. Their gifts will be reduced and some of them might be unaware of where they came from. They incarnate knowing this might happen when sent on their quest.

The ocean in the Wise One Realm sits at the foot of these gorgeous forests with the relaxing sounds of nature. Many who have incarnated from a Realm and into a human body have attempted to recreate this ambiance on Earth through their dwelling or through music and those nature sound music CD's. This takes them back to home in Heaven, even if they don't realize that's why they're listening to it.

No one is hurting anybody in the Heavenly Realms. They're also not governed by the kind of ego that human souls have. The destructive human ego that causes wars, harm, hatred, losses and early death are nowhere near a Spiritual Realm or World.

In the heavenly realms they are not chasing a pointless human job that destroys their health and relationships. They have no need for such materialism and gratification. Are human souls truly gratified with this five days a week, break my back kind of work? You make a living to survive and at the expense of selling yourself out to the kind of job where you lose yourself in it. In the process, you alienate and harm your health and relationships. Not to mention the unhappiness and unhealthy blocks that permeates and attacks your aura over a period of time.

The heavenly realms are filled with only the highest of pure love, joy and happiness. This includes rituals and parties of dance and music. All of these higher vibration spirit beings in the realms play, love, sing and dance. The music rushes out into a speaker that comes out of nowhere. It rises from the ground as the Elementals unite in telepathic harmony. They are in no need of alcohol or mind altering substances that human souls feel they require in order to reach a state of bliss. This is a beautiful uplifting natural high that is better than any drug. It occurs innately as every soul in the heavenly realms give off high vibration energy. It's in the air, in the surroundings, in the flowers, the ocean, the desert sands and every pebble within the waterfall. It's in all of the realms souls including the elementals, wise ones, angels and star souls.

Outside of the Wise One Realm and the Elemental Realm is the neighboring Desert land. Unlike on Earth where the desert temperatures have been known to be unbearable during the Summer months, in the Realms of Heaven, the temperature stays relatively the same temperature always regardless of the habitat. The realm in the desert unsurprisingly houses souls that some understand to be Aladdin Genies or desert souls.

Atlantis is considered a lost civilization that some believe existed while others believe to be mythology. Regardless of what the human soul's mind believes or doesn't believe, what appears to be Atlantis protrudes high up into the Heavens. It sits out in the distance across the ocean in the Realm world. It's strong and more vibrant than the human eye can take in. It's above the sea in the distance across from where the Wise Ones and Elementals live. The Atlantis structure stretches for miles and sits out in the distance in the ocean. Instead of being buried beneath the sea on Earth, it is alive and well above sea in Heaven. It only takes about a minute or two for a Realm spirit to reach it. The waves around it crash up with brilliant deep rose, violet and indigo blue lights. In and around Atlantis exists alien life form that glow colors which shift and change. These glowing lights fall in from above in the Heavens and sift in and out from Atlantis. The structure is made out of a variety of crystals. The energy coming off it can faint a human soul unaccustomed to its overbearing power.

As the Wise One on the other side, I stand strong at the top of the rocks where a waterfall flows freely into the clear water below. Different brightly colored lights of varying colors move about in mid-air. These lights surround some Dragonflies buzzing around. The Dragonflies, who are also part of the Elemental Realm, take a bath and play in this waterfall by flying in and out of it. The waterfall emanates crystal, light-blue, bright sparkles throughout it. It's like a curtain of sparkling light.

A help shriek from a woman cries out of the Heavens. I'm alerted to a domestic abuse situation on Earth and two very large wings shoot upward out of my back. The wings do not appear to be attached to my back. They're also made out of super bright twinkling lights. You can push your hand through it and you're still not touching it. My eyes grow serious and my hand flies into the air catching my bow and arrow that fly into it with force. The bow and arrow both radiate and give off different colored sparkled lights. I form the perfect archery warrior pose aiming the arrow straight ahead of me. With human eyes it looks as if there is nothing in front of me. From the Wise Ones eyes there is something else. My focus zooms into a suburban household on Earth where a physical dispute between two people is taking place. The focus moves the way you adjust a telescope, but this is on a larger scale. I hone in and fire my arrow into the house. Just as it lands on the roof of the house, the woman strikes back in defense against her assaulter. The door opens and the police have intervened to break up the dispute.

I look onward at the results deadly stern with a slight raise of the head. My face is attractive in this world, yet strict. I leap upward into thin air about thirty feet and then dive downward off the cliff I was standing on. As I fly down my physical figure morphs into a small meteor light colored shower. I dissolve into a light source. This light soars gracefully through the Elemental forest of bright green trees, flowers and grass. Up close this soaring light moves like a twister blazing through the Midwestern United States. Within the light, my physical form can be faintly seen. A few sparkling pixie fairies both male and female in form fly along with me. Some spirit beings morph into and stay in physical form. Their physical body may appear human, but physiologically it's not the same. This physical body on the other side cannot be harmed the way it can when living in the Earth plane.

My ray of light swoops downward landing on a galloping Unicorn that appears out of nowhere. The Unicorn emanates bright white and yellow sparkles all throughout its form as its magical hooves hit the ground without touching it. The Wise One and Unicorn travel at great speed through and out of the forest, over the white sands, and towards the beautiful ocean. The

Unicorn and the Wise One separate in their respective lights as they tap the tops of the water and continue onwards over it. Their lights intertwine and weave in and out of each other. Some of the Merfolk and dolphins leap within and around the Wise One and the Unicorn's light. They all take the time out to play and let loose. Their lights dance and leap in and out of the water creating a beautiful display of magical colors. The rays and sparkles of these lights intertwine and grow larger reaching the grand Atlantis structure. The double rays of light that embody the Wise One and Unicorn separate and shoot out around the Atlantis city. Some of the Merfolks lights shoot out to the left while others shoot out to the right circling around this magical place. The city of Atlantis glows a Godly white and yellow. It's bright enough that it reaches upward blending with the sky in a way that it's difficult to tell where this light is coming from.

The Unicorns are from the Elemental realm. They have the brightest lights that are white and gold sparkles on the other side. When they choose to incarnate as a human soul, they tend to be the stunning tan blondes you imagine on a warm beach. They're carefree and at times unsurprisingly have the qualities of a human soul born in the sign of Sagittarius, or they have Sagittarius in the top tier of their chart. The top tier of one's chart can be your Rising Sign, Moon, Mercury, Venus or Mars. Some have darker hair and may even be redheads. If they have dark hair, it may be that they have blonde hair somewhere in their human genetics tree. Even though there may be a predominant hair color, physical or astrological trait in any of the Realms, the truth is it cannot be accurately applied as a 100% given. Those in the Realms have varying hair colors for example. Wise

Ones tend to have darker hair colors, black or brown, but there are some who have incarnated with blonde hair. Elementals tend to have red hair or shades of blonde, but there are Elementals who incarnate with darker hair. When deciphering where one is coming from you investigate the whole package.

There are other planes where angels, archangels and ascended masters live. The archangels reside in the highest plane closest to God. God is a source of light that is so powerful it exists in every cell that exists in all dimensions. Departed loved ones, who are not from a realm, move into the same plane as the Realm world, but reside in a different part of that plane. The angels move about through all of the spirit dimensions including the Realm world. They appear in varying colors, lights, shapes, sizes and in physical human form. Some of the angels choose to incarnate on Earth into a human body often for the first time. They are known as Incarnated Angels. Once here and living an Earthly life, they realize how horribly difficult the Earth dimension is. They spend their human lives trying to survive and adapt which never fully works for them. They are incredibly sensitive, compassionate and giving. Many find themselves getting into co-dependent relationship connections with those who take from them.

The Merfolk have just what you would expect. They have varying shades of green, blue and white sparkles around them. The other realms such as the Incarnated Angels, Elementals and Wise Ones have different colors and shades depending on the habitat they reside in. For example, the Leprechauns, who are part of the Elemental Realm, have the green sparkles of light around them, but they also have rainbow colored lights too! This light energy emanates from their hands.

They wave their hand with a hello, and a rainbow has formed giving off an uplifting happy energy.

The Realm World is part of the Astral Plane. This is similar to the way a County in the United States is considered to be part of a State. The Realm in this scenario is the County and the Astral Plane is the State. The Realm World exists in another dimension as all of the different planes do. The furthest dimension is where the Archangels reside. It is the closest proximity to God.

The Realm dimension sits right on top of the Earth Plane. It's lowered into it, but connected to the Astral Plane dimension that overlaps that. This is why some who may be clairaudient or super in tune to Elementals may walk through a garden on Earth and hear something that isn't visibly in front of them. Crossing over back into the Spirit or Realm Plane is like walking into the next room.

It is interesting to note the way the Realm World sits within and on the Earth plane, but in a different dimension. There is a doorway and tunnel of light you pass through and you're there. The Elementals dominate the Realm Kingdom with the Wise Ones. Both the Wise Ones and Elementals are grounded closest to Earth. The Elementals and Merfolk are the closest followed by the Wise Ones. Over the course of human history, some have protested to have spotted the Elementals and a Mermaid or Merman. Some have claimed to have seen a fairy, a mermaid or even a Unicorn! Are millions of people over the course of history delusional? Or are they seeing something that is really seeping in from the Spirit World? If everyone has different degrees of psychic capabilities whether they believe in it or not, then it's not out of the question.

The Astral Plane is much like it is on Earth as far as the natural wonders go. There are oceans, mountains and deserts. Other than that detail, this is where the comparisons end. The natural wonders that exist in the Realm World and Astral Plane are mind blowing in contrast with its vibrancy.

The naturesque settings on the Earth plane are glorious. Human souls are able to create and organize some resemblance of structure. Some are artistic and gifted in the world of the arts, film, sound and stage. If those are some of what human souls can manifest and conjure up, then you can imagine what the other broader dimensions are like. It's one hundred times that and difficult to describe with a painting since nothing comes close. Your entire aura, chakras and soul are turned on and the volume is cranked up. Most human souls cannot comprehend this as they are too invested into the material world of the current Earth climate. The idea that there is no afterlife and that you're gone and that is that is quite a somber view.

My Spirit team has shown me glimpses and elements from the Realm world through visual and auditory cues, otherwise known as Clairvoyance (clear seeing) and Clairaudience (clear hearing). There is no such thing as an overcrowded population in the Astral Plane. This is what I'm calling the Realm World so the human mind can easily identify the differences between the Astral Plane and Realm World.

Back at the Atlantis structure above the Wise One figure on the other side again. I'm jumping across the top of the structure, and then into a jog literally off the cliff. I dive down from the top of the structure heading straight for the ocean water. A ray of light cocoon forms around my body. In the air, I aim the bow and arrow into the ocean and then firing immediately. The arrow shoots out in a millisecond hitting the ocean and hardening the water into a rock like tarmac below. A bright yellow light flies around the Atlantis structure. It's the Unicorn galloping around it onto the tarmac and then leaping into the air with me landing on it. We shoot across the ocean and towards the forest of greenery shared with the Elementals.

As we approach, there are hundreds of waterfalls all over the forests and atrium like settings. The original stone like structure that was originally seen by the first waterfall is not a small structure at all. It's a towering castle that shoots out into the heavens. There is a soft gold glow around it. There are dozens and dozens of varying shapes of beautiful castles spread out all over the place. The glow of the desert near the world of the Wise Ones and Elementals also glows far in the distance. What I relay from my Spirit team on the other side and what I personally believe or know are two different things. I have an analytical mind and always require proof and confirmation from my team. This is why I will double and triple check when I receive information. My job is to relay the messages and guidance they give me regardless of my own personal beliefs on any given day. What others or I take from it or do not take from it is irrelevant.

Chapter Two

Incarnating on Earth

Why did I elect to come to Earth? Why would I do that knowing of its hostility? The simple answer is there isn't much going on in Heaven. Everything is already peaceful, joyful and handed to you the second you think of it. There's not much to be done. It's already perfect in every way. This is why many from the various Realms choose to incarnate into a human body for positive benefits that also include balancing out the harsh energies of Earth.

On the other side, those in the Realms also assist certain individuals throughout the duration of that human soul's life, while others assist on bigger global issues. They may be assigned particular cases where they agree to help a certain Country or State. This entails working with a human individual in power behind the scenes with that person's guardian angel or spirit guide. This is in order to guide that person in power to do the right thing. As you can imagine this is a complicated job because they are dealing with that human soul's free will choice. These days that has a tendency to override that person from listening to their own Spirit Guide or Guardian Angel. Unfortunately, for this reason, they find it easier if they incarnate into a human life knowing that it won't be easy. They know that they can do more while on Earth than from the Other Side. There was a time when human souls were more in tune. The diets were healthier and they spent a good deal outdoors. This is where the messages from Heaven come in stronger without the distraction of the noise of the rest of the world.

There is life in other galaxies and solar systems beyond the Earth's dimension, but human souls will never find it. If they get their hands on it with their greedy ego, they will destroy it the way they are destroying much of the Earth's habitat and each other. They are not allowed anywhere near these galaxies for this reason. This is one of the things they have no control over. Earth is the kindergarten for new souls. They are surrounded by advanced and accelerated teacher souls from the various realms on the other side.

All human souls have free will choice. No one in the spirit world is allowed to intervene with that, unless you specifically grant them authority to help. You can request Heavenly assistance by calling out to them out loud, mentally or in writing. This is God's law. This free will choice prompts others to do as they please without considering the consequences. We see this is in those who misbehave or cause senseless tragedies. It is not His job to stop you from acting out. He only hopes that you wake up and do your best to be a good person.

The human soul who is making poor choices may notice a synchronicity happening in their life that is a message for them to do the right thing. They may still ignore it, but at some point will protest, "Why is this constantly in front of me?? I'm not interested!" Their ego rules the roost refusing to pay attention to heavenly guidance that will ultimately help them or someone else. The souls on the other side working the particular case may feel some measure of excitement that the individual is noticing what is being put in front of them. Yet, it's back to work in continuing to nudge and place the symbols and signs that an intelligent worldly human soul would normally pick up on. This is not to say that those who don't notice these things are not intelligent. There are a great many human souls who are in powerful human positions who are intelligent, but lacking in a connection outside of themselves that could further bring them and those around them immense joy, abundance and peace.

Your thoughts produce things on the other side much like on Earth. However on earth, the energy of your thought travels through a much denser force field making it difficult to bring abundance to you immediately. They do eventually come to fruition in some form and at some point. They are at times manipulated to an extent because earthly human souls have not mastered the thought producing process the way those on the other side do by nature. To those on the other side, it's as easy as riding a bike, brushing your teeth or washing your hands.

About 1/3 of the human souls on earth have lived in spirit form before electing to come here. The Wise

Ones of that group are masters at this manifestation process on the other side. They are also consciously or subconsciously aware that once they choose to incarnate as a human soul for one human life that the magical gifts they have on the other side will be suppressed when they arrive. It will feel as if they are putting on a big heavy, wet coat. This is why some of them have experienced feelings of being trapped. This is their soul being confined in a human body. They are not able to move freely in the way they do back home in the Realm and Spirit world. Yet, despite this the Wise Ones have been incarnating on Earth since its conception more than any other spirit being. They've enacted some of Earth's greatest inventions and knowledge to the masses.

This fight the Wise One has in the human body is spent trying to bring those heavenly gifts back out as much as possible. All human souls have this gift even the new ones regardless if they're aware of it or not. There are souls who have no belief in an afterlife and yet they are also able to manifest through the same principles. In fact, some complain that those who are not a believer seem to have things handed to them. This is because regardless of what that human soul believes is irrelevant when it comes to the manifestation process. They believe when you die, then you're gone and that's that. They have less fear involved within them that would prohibit them from attracting in their desires. Whereas someone who is a big believer, might have traces of fear or guilt that had been instilled in them by human influences. Negative feelings such as fear or guilt blocks good things from coming into your life. Corrupt souls who attract in abundance through unreliable means eventually reach a point where their luck runs out.

Human souls are immediately taught about physical survival by their peers and in their upbringing on Earth. This becomes their #1 focus while here. Subsequently, they shun the gifts that exist within them that would assist in helping them acquire the material needs they desire to live comfortably through the duration of their Earth life. Physical survival is hammered into their human psyche immediately. When they grow older they might find anything metaphysical or outside of themselves to be hogwash. Yet, they've forgot who they were when they were four years old. It was not nonsense when you were a child.

Because some Wise Ones on Earth are claircognizant and can be some of our great inventors, scientists and professors, some of them have no belief in the other side. However, what I'm told by my Guides and Angels is that this may be the case for most of their human life, yet there are blips of moments in that Wise Ones time on Earth where they are not truly an atheist, but more agnostic. They are more left brained where their mind requires concrete tangible proof of something. The Wise Ones are open to the possibility if they're not a believer growing up. They will usually go through a shift later in life where they are more open to the possibilities of the unknown.

Heaven knows that when you live comfortably without fear or worry of having your bills paid, then you have more time to contribute to helping the planet and its people in some form.

The brand new souls that are a mere seed that sparked out of the Light incarnate immediately on Earth before anywhere else. Earth is the bottom of the barrel so to speak. It's outrageously dense, volatile and dangerous. It's a playground of naughty adult kids vandalizing the planet and each other in any way they can.

Other older souls that incarnate on Earth choose to for specific purposes. This is in order to stop human ego from blowing this planet up. Some do this by saving the oceans, the animals and the Earth's habitat from destruction. Others come back here as teachers and guides in human form, since most people today have stopped listening to the other side. They are instead interested in human materialistic ego gratification, which in the end will go away, and then what are you left with?

Chapter Three

Incarnated Angels, Incarnated Elementals, and Star People

There are souls who reside in Realms or Worlds that exist in the other spirit dimensions. Some of those souls agree to incarnate on Earth into a human vessel. They may volunteer to do so or they are approached to do so. They incarnate on Earth for specific purposes or duties. This is in order to improve circumstances on this planet and its dimension. There are a variety of ways they do this that include, but not limited to assisting, guiding, teaching or protecting this planet and its souls. Most people do not listen to or follow the wisdom of something they cannot see, so those in the Spirit Worlds will come here in human form to enact these changes. Some of these souls are from a wide variety of tribes or realms on the other side. They tend to exude particular traits that are similar with that tribe. This is in the same way we come to link certain personalities with an astrological sign.

Not all human souls come from a specific realm. Some are brand new souls who start out on Earth first to have an Earthly run. They are the ones causing the most destruction. They're the innocent, newbie souls, yet they have been brought up, raised and developed by souls who allow their lower selves and ego to run the show. They raise these souls this way. Those souls take what they've learned to put it out there and so forth. What they've learned can often be things like hate, judgment and harm. They believe they are doing right, but this has caused issues on the planet. Therefore, many souls from the various realms incarnate on Earth to alleviate this energy. One soul cannot do it alone. This is why there are so many out there contributing what we can in various ways to balance out this darkness.

Those from a specific realm all have one thing in common, and that is that they are aware there is a problem here on planet Earth. They are also self aware. In addition, they have an unstoppable desire from within to correct it in some way. For some, like the Incarnated Angels, it can be simply to spread love and compassion. For others, such as the Wise Ones, it may be to teach or instill rules of etiquette. For others, such as the Incarnated Elementals, it can be to save or cleanup areas on Earth that need attention like the oceans, mountains, deserts, animals, etc.

In a sense, Earth was created to nearly resemble elements that exist in the Spirit world. These are the natural wonders around Earth. Material items like cars and overcrowded homes on top of one another are all man-made stuff. Human ego loves clutter in order to keep people feeling stifled and confused.

Every soul is here for the purpose of love. Some are here to learn to love while others are here to teach it. In the end it's all about love. All roads lead to this realization. Not all human souls are Earth Angels from a Realm, however my Guides have told me that new souls may and can evolve into a Realm depending on their spiritual growth. All souls that exist were birthed out of the Divine. Every human soul has a life purpose and mission, but it is up to them to come to terms with what that is. Some may live an entire Earthly life and yet never come to this realization. Non believers or those who have allowed their ego to rule their life become disconnected from the knowledge of where they came from due to human tampering during the development process. Regardless, they all came from somewhere.

Mediums have been conducting successful and accurate connections from the other side for centuries. They have been doing this by relaying prophetic messages about what's to come as well as messages from Departed Loved Ones. The messages and guidance would later prove true or be confirmed by the person the message is being relayed to. With that in mind, it is safe to say that they will relay messages surrounding the nature of the Spirit World and Realms.

The four central Earth Angel Realms are The Wise Ones, Incarnated Angels, Incarnated Elementals and Star People (or Star Child). Let's take a brief look at three of them in this chapter, before we move in-depth to the tribe of the Wise Ones in the following chapter and beyond.

INCARNATED ANGELS

The largest community is the Incarnated Angels. They are the most sensitive of the tribes, even though all clans have some level of sensitivity and compassion within their nature. Incarnated Angels exude *empath* and *clairsentient* traits to a high degree. Clairsentience means *clear feeling*. Incarnated Angels are Angels who chose to incarnate into a human body. Unfortunately, due to the heavy atmosphere of the Earth dimension, many of them struggle to endure their life in human form. They experience discomfort in the human body and might make statements that are along the lines of feeling like they do not belong here. Arrogant human souls easily taken advantage of them without the Incarnated Angel realizing it until it's too late. Incarnated Angels feel as if they were placed on Earth by mistake. They cannot understand who in their right mind would attempt to place a bundle of love energy into a battlefield. The unconditional love they have within them is needed in the Earth's atmosphere to temper the firing range of bullet ions that shoot out from this planet on a daily basis. This is one of the many roles of the Incarnated Angel.

They make great healers, counselors and angel intuitive spiritual readers. They love to discuss their problems with other people on a regular basis and are usually the ones you hear in an elevator talking to a friend about what someone did to them and how upset they are about it. They're chatty and will open up immediately to anyone who will listen. Some of them have a tendency to put on a little weight if they're not careful. This is usually stemming from an addiction to unhealthy foods used to create a shield of armor around their sensitive feelings.

An Incarnated Angel on Earth has the qualities of someone who only sees the love and true spirit in all souls. This can get an Incarnated Angel into trouble since they attract in and latch onto toxic human souls believing they can save them. They have co-dependent compassion for them unable to see the danger until they find that the toxic soul has pulled the rug from underneath them. Incarnated Angels are the ones that over give, but they must guard this tendency since it makes them more susceptible to being taken advantage of by other less senseless souls.

Those who have incarnated from a spiritual realm are not the ones lazily hanging around the house with no purpose. They're also not the ones that abuse or corrupt any system. They are the ones that have a huge inner calling that pushes them to accomplish something that positively benefits others. The only exception are the Incarnated Angels, who may be jobless or without drive. This isn't necessarily out of laziness. The Incarnated Angels are so sensitive that they may have low self-esteem while in a human body. Some of them might be seen as without drive, but this is because they do not always go after what they want. They feel like they're putting others out when someone offers to help them. Unfortunately, Earth is a "dog eat dog" world with struggling egos fighting to dominate. The Incarnated Angel doesn't have to suffer in a job where people are unkind. They would do well to find work that will bring out their compassionate and healing qualities. The world is slowly changing and this is much needed right now more than ever.

INCARNATED ELEMENTALS

The Incarnated Elementals are here to help the Earth's habitat. They are the ones working with animals or in jobs that are connected to nature. They would be happiest doing work such as landscape artistry, gardening, veterinarian work, joining environmental organizations, or anything that helps God's Earth in any form. You can find Incarnated Elementals working at a place where animals reside, such as a Zoo or a wildlife preserve. It is true that the Incarnated Elemental may be the one to stop mankind from locking animals up, but in the meantime they feel comfortable working close with animals even in a Zoo. They are the ones always posting stories about animal cruelty on their social networking pages. They may also blog and post about issues where harm is being caused to anything connected to nature. This is their big purpose while here.

Incarnated Elementals come from woodsy areas in the spiritual realm. When they incarnate into a human soul, some of them have the kind of features one would equate an Elemental to be. Some of the Incarnated Elementals have fairy like qualities, or resemble gnomes, elves and leprechauns. The Incarnated Elementals tend to be extroverted, bouncy and playful, although there are those who are more serious Elementals too. They have a spark and mischievous undertone to their eyes. Many of them despise living by the rules and just want life to be a big party. They're the ones who bring people together in harmony making them feel at home. They're joyful and bouncy, but if you get on their bad side, you'll meet a Dr. Jekyll and Mr. Hyde personality. They get serious and angry if someone is hurting animals, nature or the planet. They have one of the larger egos in the realm world because they are so close to the physical world.

STAR PERSON

Those from the Star Person realm are the ones that are on Earth to lend a helping hand without wanting anything in return. They're typically the quiet guy or girl at the office who keeps to themselves and yet is super hard working. No one usually knows much about him or her. Many of them light up whenever the genre of Science Fiction is brought up. They're the ones going to the Sci-Fi or Super Hero conventions. They may be some of our great inventors, filmmakers and scientists. They are usually the most technological savvy and have an understanding of the functionality and nature of gadgets. They are and were also responsible for the rise in great technology such as the inventions of tablets and mobile phones, Computers, Televisions, Movie Theater screens, etc. Star people tend to see clairvoyant images or impressions of a life they once lived on another planet at another time.

The world might consider them an odd ball or nerd, but if they look closer they'll note the genius aspect. Star People might be your helpful flight attendant or gifted scientist, to those in social power. They have the least amount of emotion or feeling of the realms and would make great politicians who are in political office specifically to enact positive change. They're not the corrupt, dodgy and non-inclusive politicians that the world is seeing these days. Star People have an unusual look to them and might appear "out of this world". They might be the woman who cakes herself in make-up, or shaves her eyebrows off and pencils it in higher. The Star Person in either gender might apply make up around their eyes to make them appear unusual. They may dress to blend into the wall or they may be the extreme opposite by dressing in bold colors. Star People, like all in the Realms, are here for a larger purpose and become aware of that at some point in their human life.

Chapter Four

The Wise One

The Wise Ones who incarnate in a human body are natural born leaders and teachers. They're the generals of an army or a soldier in combat. They are the pot stirrers that bring on significant change through their sometimes seeming aggression.

Wise One's are the darkest breed in the angelic spiritual Realm. Their presence is darker, tougher and even more sinister than any of the other realms. Wise Ones do not hold back and can be uncensoring at times. They have foul mouths cursing and cussing like sailors, but yet teach and fight in the name of the Light. Their personalities and demeanor comes off rougher around the edges than other folks. Some of them are quite intimidating in the way that they carry themselves and appear. Some are brawny and strong such as history's soldiers at war. There are the Wise Ones who might appear small, yet when you examine them closely you'll notice their body is quite strong.

When in doubt, one of the best ways to determine who is a Wise One is in their eyes. Their eyes are large, stunning, dark, intensely piercing and penetrating. Many of them never get used to others gushing over the beauty of their eyes. When some Wise Ones age in human years, they may develop significant lines under their eyes more than someone else might. You see this in the wise image of a professor or teacher. Do not be misled by the Wise Ones in human body who appear frail or ancient, as they are anything but delicate.

Wise Ones have a significant sized ego, but not quite as large as the Incarnated Elementals. They are also critical and judgmental about most everything around them. Generally the judgments are surrounding those that lack respect or are without proper etiquette. It's this kind of teaching toughness where no guff is allowed. They have no problem flipping back and forth from keeping to themselves to working independently. Hard work is a big deal for Wise Ones. They at times have opinions that they know are gold while the rest are ignored. To say they can be self-righteous at times is an understatement. "It's my way or the high way," would be a Wise One talking.

The soul of a Wise One is an innate loner who fights and hunts. They feel little to no shame or guilt in their actions or words even if it's out of line. They have a job to do and nothing will get in their way. This personality trait is part of their soul make-up and exists while living in an Earthly life.

Wise Ones are awesome manifestors, spell casters, psychics and all knowing spirits in human bodies. They will bring in and deny anything effortlessly depending on how they channel the energies. Wise Ones could be a warlock or witch type. They have a great fascination for

Wicca. They are attracted to and explore the dark arts. They also have a special affinity to movies on magic, manifestation and sorcery. This might be entertainment such as *Harry Potter, American Horror Story: The Coven, Hocus Pocus, Sword and the Stone,* or the *Chronicle.* All Wise Ones on the other side use spell casting and magic. This is regardless of what form they take and whether it is in the form of a Warlock, Knight, Witch, Wizard, High Priest or Priestess or Hunter. This is the way things work on the other side even if they do not partake in it as a human soul. A human soul would need to suspend disbelief to comprehend the ways the spirits move about on the other side. Witch or warlock can be either male or female. They incarnate from the Realm of the Wise One. I fall into the breed of the Hunter. Yet, the Hunter is still part of the tribe of the Wise Ones and has the same capabilities as the Warlock, Priest or any other element from the world of the Wise Ones.

Wise Ones also come in the guises of Church leaders such as priests and ministers. They're also the task master professors in the education system. They're usually strict, brooding, serious, but boasting of love and compassion intertwined from within. God forbid they show this! When the Wise One speaks, he means business! The Wise One can command an army of thousands, like Martin Luther King Jr. or stand on a concert stage in front of thousands in popular culture like Bono from the rock group U2. The musicians that fall into the Wise One category are the ones that have higher purposes to help humanity in some way beyond the music. Many of them tend to be the rockers while the pop stars of today are more of the Incarnated Elemental variety.

Tending to moodiness, being difficult and appearing with intense dark eyes, Wise Ones *"know it all"* and may not know how they do when you ask them. Wise Ones incarnated from the other side are Claircognizant in a bigger way than others. This is a sense of knowing the correct answers to something without any prior training. They receive heavenly guidance effortlessly through their crown chakra above their mind. They're the ones that others go to for advice or assistance. People learn to trust the Wise One as they are one of the most trustworthy people around, but just avoid getting on their bad side or rubbing them the wrong way. Those ready to move to the next plateau spiritually in their soul's growth find themselves attracted to a Wise One and take heed of their wisdom. The lesser evolved or superficial souls may feel threatened by the Wise One or find them to be dull or on the boring side. They may also find that they cannot relate to them socially or are intimidated by them. These are the human souls that are consumed by poor media and life choices. They're the ones prone to drama and gossip, which the Wise One shuts down and rarely resorts to. The Wise One has a holier than thou stance in the presence of those less evolved.

The Wise Ones are used to attracting in people from all walks of life. Many befriend them for their knowledge and what they can gain in that arena. Some of those that latch onto the Wise One develop an immediate heightened delusion that they are close best friends with the Wise One, when in reality they are mere acquaintances. Danger lies when a co-dependent human soul latches onto the Wise One for a friendship in order to simply dump their problems on them or impress them. This is a forced and unbalanced friendship where the other person is using the Wise One to pour their drama issues onto them on a regular basis, or probe them for constant help and information. The Wise One is usually hip to what is taking place and they *know* that this connection dynamic will eventually end. They are so used to stepping in to assist others with their problems, that they must guard themselves that boundaries are not crossed and friendships are not forced with them. Unlike the Incarnated Angels who will feel guilt and fear about cutting someone toxic out of there life, the Wise One doesn't observe those feelings when removing a low vibration human soul from their vicinity. The Wise One is easily irritated and rubbed the wrong way that flicking harsh energies off their shoulders is a regular occurrence. A Wise One needs to be careful on how they direct their energy, since it flows through them almost effortlessly. It might cause upsetting situations in their lives for them, or for others, when they direct and channel this energy negatively. When someone doesn't follow their lead, the Wise Ones are the souls that have the temper in the Spirit world. They have to be careful how they channel this aggression since it will create a catastrophe when intertwined with their magic manifestation capabilities. Both the Wise Ones and the Incarnated Elementals have the greater egos and temper than any of the other Realms. However, the Wise Ones have the greater tempers while the Incarnated Elementals have the greater ego and demand for attention. You would think they would go hand and hand, but they are quite different.

Wise Ones are close to and drawn to the Incarnated Elementals and vice versa. The Incarnated Elementals are on the upbeat side and drawn to the serious leadership of the Wise Ones. It is an interesting match of opposites attract. You have the outgoing or childlike

Elemental, with a darker, serious and withdrawn Wise One. A great deal of my serious love relationships have been with Incarnated Elementals! This goes without saying that some of my close friendships are with these out of sorts Elementals too. The Wise Ones bring order and discipline to the Elementals, while the Elementals help the Wise Ones relax, lighten up and enjoy life a little.

Wise Ones are attracted to darker material and even entertainment or lifestyles. It's not uncommon for them to have experimented with everything under the sun including and even fallen into addictions with drugs, alcohol, cigarettes and sex pursuits. They might also be prone to self-medicating in other ways beyond this if they can get their hands on it. They have no problem experimenting with all that life has to offer even if it's harmful. It subconsciously feeds their need to understand how something works. The colors within their soul are bright able to absorb the human experience more than any other. The addictive behavior is there under the surface, but it's not usually long lasting the way it would be with an Elemental indulging in their drink for an entire Earthly life. When Wise Ones realize their calling, they immediately pull themselves up by their bootstraps and dive in like a confident soldier. Wise Ones are the fighters, soldiers and hunters from the other side in the literal sense. Some wear the knight armor, others wear the cloak, and some carry the bow and arrow (as described in the beginning of the book). Wise Ones are the professors, the Saints, the leaders of change, the generals, sergeants, and soldier's in the army and marines in the navy. Because the Wise One's often have to be right, they might be the defiant soldier or marine. However, they are typically considered one of the best by those in charge, therefore it's overlooked. The Wise One has the stance that they have a job to do. They have no need or desire to be micro managed. With that said, most of them are entrusted with the bigger missions in combat by their superiors.

In fact some of the most notable Wise Ones are the popular Saints and Prophets in the world's history. People such as Saint Louis, who was already made King of France at the age of twelve. He also got his hands dirty by going to battle with the other soldiers. There was Saint Vladimir of Kiev in the 900 years A.D. In the beginning of his rule he was considered someone with an ugly temper and did some horrible things such as human sacrifices and obtaining hundreds of concubines. At one point he turned against paganism and went through a personal transformation that led him to be a "man of faith". His horrible reputation was quickly transformed and others began to refer to him as Vladimir the Great. The history books are filled with Wise Ones who started out with a bad reputation and who are not exactly the friendliest people on the planet right off the bat, but they end up transforming into more of a spiritual calling and following. Make no mistake that they did not necessarily change to being sweet as pie, but their fights and intense energy were transferred into more religious, spiritual and faith based fights. Wise Ones who come in the guises of Popes and Bishops would be the one granting the Saint title to the Wise One individual who has made an impact towards humanity and history.

When a Wise One enters the room, others notice. They will come off quiet, intense or with an air of superiority even though they're not trying to convey that on purpose. No one could pull off that act day after day until the end of their lifetime. It is part of their innate nature. It is how their energy light is on the other side. Those who do not know them in a personal way will immediately assume that the Wise One is conceited or icy cold. They may describe them to others by using an unpleasant curse word. As one takes the time to befriend and get to know the Wise One, they will discover they have to put in some effort since Wise Ones do not become instant friends with anybody. They have a protruding wall of distrust of others around them that must be scaled gradually over time before they open up. The opening up takes awhile and even then you feel like you don't really know them. Their opening up will be in short bursts, before they become comfortable enough to pour endless words over someone.

Those who initially had found the Wise One difficult and rough edged at the first encounter will notice a different side to them as they become closer. They will realize they've made an error in judgment and that the Wise One is indeed one of the coolest and most loyal people they know. They come to find that the Wise One is charismatic and warm when they're called to engage in social situations and put on that politician energy. Most of the Wise Ones personality is of a dark, depressed energy keeping to themselves. This is not out of shyness, but out of disinterest in superficial small talk. They dislike idle chit-chat and gossip and will rarely strike up a conversation out of the blue with someone in an elevator unless they're asked a question. In fact, they may step away from strangers in an elevator or anywhere for that matter. They want the bullet points when someone is addressing them or in a meeting, but when you ask them a question, they will give you a novel of an answer.

A Wise One might be pushed into the role of giving speeches rallying up the masses with their work, but some of them are uncomfortable on a stage. If this is the case, they may have other astrological influences that point to this. There might also have been crucial incidents that happened within their upbringing and development of their current life as a human soul that resulted in a fear of the stage. These things play a part within the Wise One who might be uncomfortable getting in front of the masses. You must strip the soul of their human ego learning's to get to the heart of their realm. You're looking at what they tend to exude overall.

Wise Ones often feel gypped that human souls have lied and caused so many preventable issues. Mankind has turned others against spiritual belief concepts to no belief at all with great success! This is one of the reasons Wise Ones incarnate. They are not instructing and authoritative out of malice, but to correct the bully's behavior.

Wise Ones either appear much older than their years or much younger than their years. They rarely look exactly their age. In fact, throughout most of their life they may comment that others come off shocked when they find out how old they truly are. When I was 21, I looked like I was 12. When I was 35, people thought I was 24 and in College. The Wise Ones have an interesting appearance where there age is difficult to detect. The Wise Ones who have always appeared much older than their years gives them the look of many lifetimes etched into their face. Those who have always appeared younger than their human age have that elusive, mysterious quality of centuries gone by. They fit the image of the vampire, which is another favorite mythological character of a Wise One. If vampire,

41

Count Dracula, were real he would be a Wise One. He's got the gothic darkness in him. He's got the romanticism in his search for love and the dangerous anger when crossed.

Although a Wise One may come out of hiding to rally up the masses when it's called for, generally they are more on the reclusive side. Wise Ones may be accused of being cynical. This is someone who has distaste for the direction humankind has been going in. The Wise Ones may appear misanthropic, but in truth they have exceedingly high expectations from human souls. They see humanity as a whole has not got their act together after all of these centuries. They're still fighting and demanding attention or paying attention to less important causes. They believe humanity doesn't have a high standard of professionalism and decorum in their day to day connections with other human beings. Wise Ones are the taskmasters and disciplinarians after all and when a student defies their instructions, this will rise the Wise One into irritation. They will more or less cast that soul out of their vicinity. This makes them seem anti-social at times, yet they are far from it. They simply direct and channel their energy towards those souls who are ready to listen. They do not direct their energy towards anyone or anything that doesn't need to be.

This detached coolness can turn off, attract or repel other human souls. Lower energies are uncomfortable with someone who is not like the others. Wise Ones do not refuse conformity on purpose. They have lived through so many lifetimes and in the Spirit World that most of that nature is engrained into their human soul.

Where an Incarnated Angel may find it difficult to say "no" or will go out of their way to assist most anyone in need, the Wise One and the Incarnated Elementals with their ego expect others to work for it. The Wise Ones specifically don't have a problem saying no, even if they did in adolescence. Once they come into their own, if they hadn't at an early age, they will start asserting themselves. Wise Ones have a fine tuned detector where they can immediately tell if someone is of honor or not within a minute or two. I know very few Wise Ones who have actually had constant run-ins with someone of less integrity. Usually the calls I get from being slighted by others on a regular basis come from other human souls, Incarnated Angels, Star people, and Elementals.

Wise Ones on the other side are the many that greet the soul who is crossing over from the Earth plane. The soul has questions within them, which the Wise One on the other side answers. Family and friends greet the departed soul on the other side. It's the Wise One who is there with them to chime in and answer the questions from the newly departed soul. The Wise One helps them make amends for crimes they've committed on Earth, along with Archangel Jeremiel, and that soul's Guide and Angel.

When I asked why souls are tested at times. My team said, "If we don't test them, then how will they learn?" This is much like when you go to school and have to take a test in order to gain knowledge. Who do you think is executing these test orders? Many come from the Realm of the Wise One.

Wise Ones will have most of the traits discussed in this book if not all. If you find that you fall into maybe half of the traits without question, then it's possible you fall into one of the many blended realms that have some Wise One in them. For instance, the Mystic Angel is half Wise One and half Incarnated Angel.

Chapter Five

The Fighting Nature of the Wise One

There are a great many books and resources that contain vast information of knowledge in terms of esoteric, philosophic and metaphysic concepts. Many teachers and guides born into a human body from the world of the Wise Ones on the other side are filtering these into public view. There are so many of them because not everyone will pick up the common message from just one source. Not everyone is attracted to the same teacher. Some prefer the way one Teacher instructs something as opposed to another Teacher. Others like to get all points of view from several or many. What matters is that they are being reached. People are waking up and realizing that the old ways of the dark ages have no value. Everyone is exhausted over the way things were and are. They are worn out from all of the negativity and hateful ways of other people. Those who are evolving realize that it's draining and they no longer want to be a part of it. You cannot live like that anymore. Every soul wants love, happiness, abundance, joy and peace. Many of the current human souls have been moving into a higher frequency where they belong.

Tantrums are being thrown in the process of this change by lower souls in the human body. This comes mostly from the souls who are newly here or who are repeatedly sent here to make amends for their lifetimes of horrible actions on others. They are used to things being a certain way due to what history and society insists on, but that no longer works and more people are growing hip to that. It's too negative and has no basis in reality. It comes from fear, which is not real. Baby souls are easy to spot. They're the ones operating from more ego than anyone else. They put out the most toxic and negative energy into the Earth's atmosphere. They can be those who spend their entire Earthly life watching trash gossip T.V. and contributing nothing towards humanity in the way of love or joy. Partaking in time wasting gossip sucks the life force out of you.

They can be someone who commits repeated violent crimes only to see their life end short. They are the ones who do everything in their power to push down and harm other souls in some way. What's perpetuated and force fed in the media also needs to change. They are one of the biggest culprits, until they wake up and decide to change things positively. This will happen as more souls from the Realms move into media positions over the course of Earth's future.

This isn't to say that those from the various realms do not act out from ego or throw a tantrum, but typically their anger is over the poor treatment of other people, or the aspects of this planet that are being destroyed. The

Incarnated Elementals and Wise Ones tend to showcase this anger the most. They direct it outwardly while the Incarnated Angels and Star People internalize it more than direct it.

Wise Ones are prone to temper tantrums, but usually the anger is pretty contained. It's simmering underneath the surface ready to erupt when pushed. The strong willed expressive nature of the Wise One is engrained in his soul's DNA. When things are not running smoothly, they will make it known. Silencing the Wise One is never a good idea. If they do not retaliate right then and there, they may sneak up behind you like the image of the Dark Knight from the Batman movies. It may seem like Wise Ones are just angry curmudgeons, but this is far from the truth. They expect the best out of souls knowing the soul is capable of it. If the soul wasn't lost and mired in their culture's superficiality, then they would be capable of great magnificence. To say Wise Ones are not judgmental is an understatement, but their criticisms usually come from the place of a Teacher or Instructor cracking the whip to snap someone into shape. This is why many Wise Ones make great Military Sergeants. They do not have time for the gossip kind of criticisms that sell trashy tabloids. Their judgment is towards those who continue to read those tabloids keeping them in business and buying into the hype.

The Wise One can be someone like Anna Wintour, the Editor of Vogue who runs a tight ship and has a keen eye for fashion. She was fictionally portrayed in the movie, "The Devil Wears Prada". To some circles she's considered the Ice Queen, but to those she allows to get close to understand where her warmth lies. Wise Ones are all about taking care of business and do not have time for idle chitchat. They expect you to be on time and do your job without being told.

It's undoubtedly known that a great many human souls are awakening to a spiritually based path. Some are finding less interest in the rigid doctrine of certain religions that enforce punishment on innocent souls. Those who come from the realms are all contributing to this movement. We've been asked to come here for this purpose. Millions are needed to usher the way and counteract the antagonistic energy being enacted on other people. Those in all realms find this barbaric behavior of the harm done to human beings by others greatly unacceptable. We've been coming here in great numbers since the turn of the 20th century and beyond to enact these changes and make a difference in a way that awakens and reopens the hearts of other souls. Those from the realms have been incarnating over the centuries. This is the first time in history that we are seeing an even larger percentage than ever before of these incarnations.

Everyone wants peace on Earth. Everyone wants love. Even the most hardened human soul craves it somewhere inside of them. Somehow they've taught each other to lose their way. Negativity is a nasty influence that plagues the planet. We can all be guilty of it on occasion, but in some circles it is spread like mad wiping out any hope for peace, love and joy to enter the equation.

Wise Ones do not pretend to be Earth Angels as they go to battle when it's required of them. The mighty warrior of God governs their daily security. Archangel Michael. He is someone Wise Ones on the other side communicate with regularly. He oversees all warriors of the Light, Indigos and Wise Ones. He is the general and we are the soldiers he supervises. We do whatever we need to do to defeat and correct anything or anyone of a lower energy. An Incarnated Earth Angel may send positive loving vibes and compassion to someone exuding a lower energy. The Wise Ones dive into battle with that energy in order to extract it the same way Archangel Michael extracts all lower energies with his sword of light. This is why those souls are called a Warrior of Light. The Wise Ones fall into this branch of soldiers for Heaven. A Warrior of Light can be anyone from any realm. They can be an evolving human soul who has incarnated in their first Earth run.

Every now and then someone of a lower energy sneaks into the vicinity of a Wise Ones area. They might be someone who uses God's name to step over the line and behave badly or that person may be a bully who is hurting or harming another life force. The Wise One has a hardcoded etiquette rule that any antagonism results in immediate ban, extrication and blocking. There is no room within the Wise One's walls for someone who allows their ego to govern their life full time. For some of the Wise Ones, it's a silent removal the way you move through your house with a broom. You sweep the dirt out gracefully moving from room to room without so much as a word. You toss the broom aside and exit your house calmly. Sometimes the Wise One might say a word and often times they do. This does not make the Wise One angelic even if there are dozens of security angels around them. These security angels are part of their Spirit team on the other side assisting them on their mission. They are the many Spirit Guides and Angels that move into the vicinity of the Wise One in human form. Wise Ones are trained to stay focused on any purpose they're given. This includes their human soul purpose, even if that means they have to be tough and play bad cop. They play bad cop very well and anyone who knows them personally will graciously confirm this. Look at some of our iconic religious and philosophical figures. They rarely bend from a hardcoded rule instilled within them to improve someone.

Wise Ones work and fight for the light and take out lower energies execution style. This is one of their many roles and jobs. They also infuse God's love energy into the souls who are straying from the right path, but are good people. Wise Ones are the protector of good-hearted souls and those who are bullied, pushed down or turned against. They are God's foot soldiers against those who are not of high integrity. The slaying list of the Wise One includes those who are rude and without proper etiquette. Wise Ones have a bit of cockiness surrounding them much like the Archangel Michael. Archangel Michael has no problem taking a break and strutting around like a peacock as he displays his vibrant colors of light. The Wise One's arrogance is no different as they move about their endeavors with unwavering confidence.

The Wise One's jobs on earth and on the other side often entail creating and protecting its area. The area around them is considered a sanctuary of peace, harmony, enlightenment, joy and uplifting optimism. In the Wise One Realm, they are the protectors of all the Realms that blend in with one another. There are warrior soldiers guarding these gates ready to take action on anyone or anything that sadly and unsuccessfully attempts to get in. Wise Ones have a zero tolerance policy for that on the other side and in human form.

The Wise One's motto is that you spend your quality time on things that revolve around LOVE.

Wise Ones are susceptible to antagonism because their work can be powerful, out of this world or ahead of its time regardless of the year it is on Earth. They often come off more advanced than the current generation that exists at the time of the Wise One's incarnation as a human soul. They have a persuasiveness about them that brings in their fair share of opposition. Think of the Apostles that followed Jesus who were crucified for supporting his spiritual work. The Wise One knows their guidance is of truth. This confidence or "know it all" aura about them rubs lower energies the wrong way. It makes the ego feel subconsciously threatened and secondary. It's not the Wise Ones intention to come off like an oppressor at times, but they were born this way out of the light of God. They are sometimes silenced for their own protection since they sometimes don't have a filter. They see circumstances through Heaven's eyes, even if they are not a believer of an afterlife. This takes on a whole new perspective for them when it comes to the day-to-day grind of the mundane world. The absurdity in certain hostile behaviors in humankind is perpetually on their nerves. Naive souls lose out from the Wise Ones heavenly benefits due to ignorance and fear.

Some Wise Ones rule with an iron fist. When someone displays harsh antagonism or energies, then that soul has just entered the viper's nest. It is not enjoyable to be in the boxing ring with a Wise One when you overstep your boundaries. The Wise One will confront you about it just before they give you the ultimate axe. All souls must be responsible for their actions and their words. Displaying this type of energy sparks fury out of the Wise One who never overlooks the need to correct someone. A Wise One may reduce bosses to tears in a fit of temper. This is to illustrate that when you attempt to mess with the structure of light that is around this world or every living thing, then the Wise One expects you to accept the consequences.

A Wise One is strong enough to take on someone's lower energy and swat them away as if it were an annoying fly. This is regardless of whether or not the Wise One finds this enjoyable too. Whereas an Incarnated Angel may be reduced to tears or want to give up after experiencing the harsh cruelty of another. The Wise Ones are the opposite in that they pull their armor up immediately and shatter that cruelty into a billion pieces. It fuels them rather than crushes them. It's like a moth heading directly into a light that causes it to crash and burn up into a flame. An Incarnated Angel had continuously witnessed this fury from a Wise One and said, "You don't take anything from anyone. How I wish I was like that."

Archangel Michael explained to me once that the people who antagonize and bully others because of their differences are what God considers *inhumane.* He sees some of his own children as inhumane? This is like any parent who has a rebellious child who acts out in a repeated tantrum causing problems to everyone around them. They can be what some see as lost causes. There is no room for that in anyone's life. Keep that stuff out and in your home that is plagued with dark energy because of your actions and thoughts.

Dealing with narcissistic souls can be fun. They are everywhere aren't they? It's a lower energy. It's someone operating from the ego full time. Sure we all have moments where our ego comes out and rules the roost, but someone who is spiritually connected is aware when that happens and shifts the vibration. The average person is not aware of doing this. This is seen in those causing corruption in the political arenas. They are too absorbed in the material world to notice anything outside of that. This is all they were taught growing up and through their developmental years. Their soul has forgotten that none of that is real and will eventually go away.

The movie, *Erin Brockovich*, is based on the Wise One of the same name, Erin Brockovich. Erin fits the bill of the Wise One nature standing up to the big guys. She is a strong willed fighter intending to make a right out of a wrong. A divorced mother of three young kids and struggling to find work, she finds her calling in the legal sphere by Heavenly fate. It was divinely guided to her life purpose. She received an inner tugging to uncover the corruption happening within a corporation that was poisoning and murdering off an entire community of people. Naysayers and corporate thugs would harass and attempt to stop her. This does not stop the Wise One who goes after a cause with great veracity. There is no stopping them from their purposes. Any doubts that arise within them do not have anything to do with a lack of ability. The doubts would be that they're not seeing any positive return, investment or attention surrounding their fight, cause or interest. Even when experiencing doubts, the Wise One still does not give up or stop.

Erin, like many other Wise Ones, is known to have a colorful palette that is often sprinkled with curse words. When I first started writing spiritually based books, we had to ensure that the curse words were removed to ensure it could be read by all audiences. Because I grew up using curse words so frequently, it would fly out without me be being aware of it.

The Wise One is much like an astrological water sign. Water signs that are evolved tend to be the most wise and connected to things beyond. Water has the power to erode the toughest material including rock. Water, just like the Wise One, turns to ice when cold and into a hurricane fury when angry. This is sometimes seductive and other times callous. Having a water sign in the top tier of one's chart doesn't necessarily mean someone comes from the Wise One realm or any realm for that matter. In this case Erin Brockovich has her Sun sign in a Water element.

The Erin Brockovich movie is an inspirational story of a Wise One coming from nothing and taking down the big guys. Erin has a special affinity to Environmental causes that she picked up from her Wise One connection with the Elementals. It may seem confusing that a Wise One is taking on Environmental causes when that is typically the role of an Elemental. The difference is that an Incarnated Elemental's sole cause and happiness is the environment and with animals, while a Wise One may have other fights beyond just the environmentalism. The Wise Ones and Incarnated Elementals have numerous similarities due to their living and working with one another on Earth and on the other side. Their differences are apparent. The most basic is in their eyes. The Incarnated Elementals have a spark or mischievous look to their eyes, while the Wise Ones have dark, deep and intense eyes.

Every human soul has the power to contribute something important towards humanity. If you feel strongly that something is wrong and needs to be righted, then this is a clue to move into position and make it happen.

Wise Ones, you are not unnoticed by Heaven! Keep doing your work and do not concern yourself with the negative attention it might attract or the lack of attention. Have honor and be of integrity. This is your true nature.

The Wise One in me said, "My soul acts as a mirror aimed at humanity. When someone is kind, then I'm kind. When someone is angry, then I'm angry. There is a catch though in the way I was designed. When love is exuded, I magnify that ten times. When anger is exuded, I also magnify that ten times. This makes me dangerous depending on what human souls display around me. I give out, what is given, but even more so. The colors on my soul's palette are vivid, more contrasted able to handle and absorb more than the average soul. Some might see this as a gift, but I've mostly seen it as a curse. You try absorbing every abnormality around you at a heightened degree every second and see how you feel."

Some Wise Ones feel like they're putting energy into a lost cause and that humanity is heading for destruction. Some of them have flung their hands in the air threatening to stop their life purpose believing they're not creating a dent in the world. Others wonder if they're giving and contributing enough service towards humanity.

My main instructor guide, fellow Wise One, Saint Nathaniel has stepped in with a message for them:

"You are giving more of the service than you realize, dear one. Do not allow your lower self to get in the way of your life's path and cripple your thoughts with unnecessary worry. It is not real and has no basis in the reality that you as a human soul understand. You have

come so far and are where you need to be more than you realize. There's nothing special you need to do to get to this place you seek, because you are there now in this moment. You are doing the work. You will continue to expand what you intended to. This is by being the truest you, and allowing your higher soul's self to govern your world. Only then are you present and in the space you thrive for. You do not need to search for this beacon. You are in the zone and in the vortex of where you as a Wise One function best."

A universal issue is the masses of souls fighting against the current to survive, to accomplish, to achieve and obtain. Sure we create some of the rock and roll, but not always. Sometime you're minding your own business, staying out of the way, and a lower energy enters your vicinity attempting to upset your Zen. Know that the work you do is needed. Your Spirit team of Guides and Angels understand that you might sometimes fall into the heavy intensity of the day-to-day grind. This causes confusion and all sorts of unpleasant stuff.

Wise One, Mother Teresa, had doubts and confessed to wanting to throw in the towel at times. It's understood that it can be frustrating when you're trying out new avenues of bringing good stuff to others, and not getting enough feedback or validation on it. You are touching more lives than you're aware of in those instances, even if it's not being acknowledged or returned. The free stuff you do counts as part of your *giving* in the *giving and receiving* equation. This is keeping all aspects of you balanced.

Wise Ones have this weighty somber feeling in regards to humanity. Sometimes they feel like there is no hope for humanity, but they know they still have a job to do. They do not take this job lightly. A Wise One once joked in their typical crass manner regarding the state of Earth. "Heaven is much better than this dump." They sometimes appear together on all levels, yet still carrying the heavy burden of the world's pain.

They do what they have to do with love in hopes it will raise at least one person's consciousness. If you want something bad enough, and deep enough, then you'll get it. If every cell within your body is filled up with this determination and passion for something, then you will achieve it. I've always received what I wished and asked for. Later I'm complaining that I made a mistake, but I did technically ask for it. You have to discover the truth on your own. Eventually there is a point where your guides refuse to tell you the ultimate outcome of a situation. We're not intended to be constantly living in the future. We have to live life and gain experiences in order to come to the ultimate truth on our own.

My life purpose has always surrounded taking charge, teaching or instructing in some form. Typically it's through the written word since that can travel around the globe much more quickly and is accessible. It will always be available long after I've departed from this plane again. Ultimately the main instructions are messages from Heaven in regards to the betterment of humanity. Often times there are no mincing words. Some of my ways or words might be seen as harsh, but hopefully they are bathed in compassion. Those who understand or pick up on it feel empowered and inspired instead of turned off. I didn't come here to mess around and was entrusted with this mission and goal. Nothing can or has ever swayed me. I've had critics, but I pay no mind and stay focused on what's important and on what I need to do. If that swayed me, then they would've just got someone else for the gig.   I have a responsibility and made a prior agreement to this. I've been acting as a vessel for as long as I can remember. I was four years old and already moving around with an underlying sense of confidence in knowing and understanding things that were beyond my years.   It quickly headed in that direction as far as work and life purpose goes.

Chapter Six

The Wise One Teacher

Many Wise Ones enjoy writing, teaching, communicating, inspiring, empowering and motivating. They find a way to incorporate those qualities into their career, pursuits and life purposes. The Wise One is built with the inner dialogue mantra that says, "As long as I stay focused on what I'm here to do, then the rest of the triviality that shows up in my daily life has no value." There's a rush or high to this work that uplifts and molds the Wise One. This same feeling is transferred to the one they're directing the information to.

This is your life and you have to live it for yourself. It is understood that souls are living in situations where there are strict human-made traditional rules. A Wise One does not subscribe to this sort of order and cannot comprehend it. Where the Wise One has come from in the Realm world resides another perception beyond what is understood by human souls. They are disconnected from the rigidness that man-made tradition sometimes forces upon others. Tradition is good to an extent since it creates some measure of structure so the human soul isn't floundering all over the place. It can stall or prevent someone from succumbing to an addiction. On the extreme side, with no room for expression and movement, this takes away the free will choice that human souls were granted by God. Wise Ones understand the human reality that exists, but it is not the real reality they know of.

A Wise One can be a rebel that defies rules regardless of who it hurts. They have the stance that says, "This is my life and I live it for me". You must do the same if you want to find true happiness. This is pending that as long as it doesn't hurt someone or destroy that person's free will. Utilizing compassion can be a struggle for some Wise Ones since they have this serious and strong warrior energy about them.

Another clue that you may have a Wise One around you is they tend to be long winded! They are the friend that has the tendency to write long emails, or leave lengthy voicemails and texts. Sometimes these notes have an underlying teaching message within them. They are knowledgeable on almost any topic, that you must be careful asking them a question. You'll get a novel for a response! Wise Ones have tons of information filtering through their crown chakra on a daily basis. Only those ready for the information the Wise One has to relay are able to dive into it and absorb it. Having a Wise One around is much like being in an advanced class for exceptional students. This leaves others feeling confused as to the meaning of their work. The Wise One can be long winded on the phone, email or in a seminar giving a speech. They're the teacher in photography class who would drone on and on for hours over the complexities of the camera. If they are an author, then that means they are teacher to whoever picks up their books.

Wise Ones are the over achievers. This may have been present when they were the smart kid growing up who was known as the *know it all* kid in grade school. On the flip side, if the Wise One wasn't the straight A student in school, they were the over achiever and straight A student in life! They are the ones that others have said, "Wow, you've accomplished so much!" Wise Ones carry out whatever they set their minds to. There is no such thing as failure to them. If they want something or need to accomplish something, no one and nothing will stop them. They will run over whoever and whatever in order to achieve this. They do not avoid making a move because they feel they're not qualified. If they have some reservations or fears, which are innately taught growing up, their Wise One nature usually rises above that feeling and does it anyway. The Incarnated Elementals have some measure of this attitude, but they are the ones that express doubt and reservation with themselves before the Wise One does. Yet, they have the larger ego with the Wise One having the larger temper. An Incarnated Elemental may dive into something without fully thinking it through, while the Wise One will be exacting and plotting while weighing the pros and cons before they carry out their intention. If a Wise One is talking about undertaking something of importance to them, then you can be sure that eventually it will come to fruition. Whereas the Elemental may talk about something and not always carry it out.

As a Wise One, I'm a writer and storyteller first and foremost. I infuse the wisdom, guidance and messages from my Spirit team into whatever I'm writing about in my books. I also relay their messages and weave it into sentences when speaking with others at times. This is without telling the person where the message came from. It will be worded so that a reader might grasp the value. Anyone in passing on the street or whom I have crossed paths with may be privy to something important said. I'm conservative in the way I relay information to someone, as it's not my place to interfere in someone's life or free will choice. It's also against God's law to interfere without someone specifically coming to you for your advice and assistance. I've had others volunteer advice without knowing me. Although I'm aware they mean well and it isn't done with malice, I know that they do not understand this basic etiquette concept.

There is great joy and bliss attached to my work as a Wise One. A good deal of the information I relay is filtered through me via *clairaudience* (clear hearing) and *claircognizance* (clear knowing) channels predominately. Once in that frequency a soaring feeling takes over my soul. There is a release of any lower-self element within the human part of me when that information comes in. The additional high is discovering that others are moved or assisted in a positive way through my work. I'm well aware that it's benefitting others too. I feel most at home doing it more than anything else in the world. There is absolutely no feeling of doubt existing within me when it comes to my work.

I knew when I was sixteen that I would be writing books. It soon grew to be professionally in a bigger way by the time I reached my mid to late thirties. What's ironic is that I've always been doing this, but the audience that is responding to it has been gliding upwards. I knew from an early age that I would write books, tell stories and weave humanity messages from spirit and Heaven into all of my books. This includes my horror book, "Paint the Silence." I've discovered that others have reacted and responded to all of it in overflowing positive ways. It truly is making a difference in some people's lives. If it were just one person who gained something that shifted their perspective in a way that enhances their life, then the Wise One has done their job.

Pluto moves into a Square with the Pluto placement in your birth chart around age 35. It stays there until about age 40. This contributes to you going through a major transformation between ages 35-40. Some have called this the mid-life crises, but it really isn't since humankind is living longer than they were years ago. You are making serious evaluations about where you are at in your life and where you are going. You are hopefully getting to a place of finding that groove with great confidence. When someone is always resorting to planetary talk, you may be talking to a Wise One! Wise Ones have come in the guises of some of our notable astrologers and scientists after all. They were people such as Alan Leo who was considered the astrologer who revived the craft. Or the scientist, Johannes Kepler, who brought planetary motion studies to the masses.

Please don't mistake that we're talking you into something or talking you out of something. If you're a strong willed soul yourself, then you know what you crave. You have free will choice to decide for yourself what is best for you. This is in keeping that you remember that you're living this life for you.

Chapter Seven

The Critics and Sensitivity of the Wise One

When the Wise One speaks up, which is often, they attract in the occasional negative words and criticisms of others. They take in a lot before they become the slightest bit affected. Some of them may have had a rough and abusive upbringing in their human life that gave them the added thick skin and street-smart toughness that is the all-encompassing Wise One. They don't take negative words and criticisms too much to heart, because any negative criticisms they receive in their life is mostly based on myths according to them. Just because it has truth within the attacker's ego, doesn't mean it is true. The Wise One might be irritatingly superior, but they are generally right on the mark.

When the Wise One lashes out on such a person, it isn't necessarily out of a sensitive reaction, but because they are going to correct the person's behavior. It would be unwise for a Wise One to not address someone who is behaving in a sadistic manner. This is permanently embedded into their soul's DNA. They know that critics do not always know what they are talking about. The Wise Ones have a highly tuned in psychic antennae. They are able to sift quickly through the words or statement someone made and flag all of the untruths. They are gifted detective sleuths and will uncover how the critic is wrong or out of line. If you're not a Wise One, you may have a Wise One friend who goes to great lengths in proving that the callous soul who is doing the attacking is incorrect.

Instead of having an understanding about it, the Wise One is pushed to anger, or they are filled with annoyance that the critic didn't get the point. Remember, they are the disciplinarians from the Light. You recall that one teacher in school who was so hard on a student who wasn't grasping what the teacher was instructing. They will be aware that it's not the compassionate way to go, but once again they pay no mind as they have a job to do. This inner goal takes precedence over anything else. Wise Ones you must always attempt to use compassion as much as possible in your dealings with others.

The Wise One is often dealing with someone who is attacking them for something in their work, something they've said or who they are in general. The opinion of the critic was not asked for and it's against the humane law to bully and cut someone down because you do not understand it or them. In the Spirit World, the Wise One is not around lower energies or critics. It's accepted and known who they are, but in the Earth plane they're dealing with some who are baby souls full of fits of ego and repressed rage. The baby souls speak out of naivety. They are unversed in the topic they're commenting on. Instead they resort to going with the not thought out point-of-view. They'll use the same rhetoric that other lesser-evolved souls have taught them instead of doing the work and diving in deeper to uncover the real truth. They appeared out of nowhere and took it upon themselves to approach you and attack. When this is the case, compassion gets thrown out the window for a Wise One. They're the solider angels after all and will come off diplomatic and authoritative when making their point. This doesn't mean they resort to physical violence although possible, but they do use words as weapons. Because of this there are others who find them to be too hard or intolerant when it comes to certain things.

What the person is saying doesn't have anything to do with the Wise One. If they knew the Wise One personally they wouldn't be saying it at all. It's almost as if they're talking about someone else. Whatever the Wise One has been saying or has done flies right over the critics' head. Wise Ones don't have the time to break it down for those who don't get it. Some may choose to ignore it rather than lash out. This is because they're likely overloaded with other fights that take precedence over someone they deem insignificant.

Negative criticism usually comes from someone who is jumping the gun and simply not understanding the point. It's a given that not everyone will understand you or your work. Everyone has free will to think and speak for themselves. Sometimes it boils down to the saying that says if you don't have anything nice to say, then don't say anything at all. If you don't understand something, you ask, you don't attack. Usually when someone's vibration has dropped or is low to begin with, the etiquette rule in being good-natured doesn't exist in their energy field. What the Wise One has said triggers upset in that person. The underlying upset has something to do with something else within the attacker that is unresolved and has absolutely nothing to do with the Wise One's words. The Wise Ones are movers and shakers with their language. They can easily rile up someone else's rigid ego.

Wise One's have the stance that their work is not up for debate. They're so used to lower energies attempting to challenge them in battle that they find it takes too much time away from more important causes. An evolved Wise One steers clear of drama and stays focused on the work.

Wise Ones have always been highly tuned in and sensitive to every nuance around them. Even though they're sensitive, there is that fighter nature that exists as well. It's an unseen soldier like force that holds onto the reigns of this sensitive part within them. They don't have a problem correcting someone or righting a wrong. It's an interesting dichotomy having the opposing factors of sensitivity and warrior nature.

The souls from the various Realms who have incarnated into an Earth life may find that in general they are naturally sensitive to people's energies. For me, I can't be around huge groups of people for too long. I have to take off pretty quickly. When I'm in that, it feels like claws digging into me from all around. It's a horrible uncomfortable feeling absorbing everybody's stuff all at once. Obviously there are places you have to go where there will be more people than you can handle. Perhaps a concert or a theme park, however that's not something I do regularly anyway. I don't stay in crowded areas for long. If I'm going outside, I have to ensure that the shield around me is impermeable. There is a mental preparation process that takes place for those instances.

Close friends who have been around me forever already act accordingly without anything being said. For example, if we're meeting at a restaurant, they make sure there's an out of the way table. If there is a harsh energy around us, they can read it just by looking at my face and my sudden discomfort. It's always been like that, but I've noticed the days I'm more in tune, the more this is aggravated.

My late teens and into my early 20's were bathed in drug and alcohol addictions. This is another side effect to being a Wise One in a human body. The Wise One resorts to regular uses of dangerous addictions. This is by doing everything to escape the heightened stimuli of everything around them. Instead of seeing it as a blessing, I saw it as a curse. Luckily, that didn't last that long. From as early as a child, I was already guided to healthier forms of eating and physical exercise. There was also an unseen and unspoken inner drive to accomplish my life purpose while I'm here. This still stands today and existed even when I was consumed in addictions.

In my late teens and into my early 20's, I'd use a narcotic drug and then chase it with carrot juice. I was consciously aware that what I was doing was not okay. Instead of embracing, nurturing and properly caring for the sensitivity within me, I searched for ways to cover that part up. What happened was that it was too quiet and I could no longer hear the guidance of my Spirit team. When I detoxed and cleansed my soul and body, the voices from my Spirit team grew louder. The volume was cranked up. I learned to use this to my advantage instead of hiding it. If I did not rise above it, then I would've end up checking out of this Earthly life early.

All the encouraging circumstances in my life have been Spirit guided, because I didn't grow up in a community or family that observed healthy eating habits. It was the messages fed to me to go for this instead of that. The trajectory of my life to date has been a series of steps climbing upward. There's no doubt or denying that.

Having heightened sensitivity is common amongst those who enter into a human body from a Realm. Wise Ones who work as Mediums or Psychics have a heightened open awareness to circumstances outside of themselves. They have *clair* channels that are psychically tuned up. When you have opened *clair* channels, you become easily worn down after being in an environment of harsh people. It's also common for some Wise Ones, and others in the Realm world, to have a higher level of agoraphobia than a new oblivious soul would have. The clinical definition of agoraphobia is someone with an irrational fear of places where an abundant amount of people congregates. This definition has an element of truth to it. Those who have *clair* channels that bounce off the scales are in tune to what's around them. They absorb the energy of other human souls and this wreaks havoc on their internal system. For that matter, they may become agoraphobic and refuse or avoid going to places where it will be crowded.

If you fall into this description, you could very well have incarnated from a specific Realm on the other side. Those who have incarnated here from a specific Realm have a higher sensitivity. The Incarnated Angels sensitivity pushes them into feeling sorry for themselves or as a victim reduced to tears. Wise Ones sensitivity prompts them to agitation where they pull up the invisible armor ready for battle.

Archangel Michael is someone I have been working and communicating with on a daily basis for years. My agoraphobia became easier to manage as he shields me regularly. I follow his lead on where and when to go to certain places, who to avoid and who is safe. Archangel Raphael guides me to natural herbs and products that assist in tempering this anxiety. The same way a celebrity will avoid going to a popular busy promenade where they will be seen and bothered, the Wise One observes the same life choices. There are certain things I do not and cannot do unless I want to be attacked by the onslaught of harsh energies. My life choices are different than the average person because of this. Those who are sensitive and well in tune can relate. The racing of the cars on the road with erratic human souls in control of these machines is a contributor to the harsh energy as well. They rush around in a hurry and ready to run anyone over in their way. This is felt by a sensitive. If you fall into this type of sensitivity, then call on and work with Archangel Michael and Archangel Raphael daily.

A sensitive knows not go to places that you know will be taxing energetically if possible. You're not going to go to an amusement park in the middle of Summer on a weekend, even if family members and friends are going. You would go on a Tuesday during low season when you know it won't be crowded. When I go to a restaurant with a friend or friends, they will ensure we're not sitting at a table in the middle of the room, but in the darkest corner. If a place is slammed with people, we go somewhere else, while the average person would sit and wait. I don't go grocery shopping in the middle of the day on a weekend. I either go first thing in the morning or at night when the crowds have died down. I don't go to the crowded more popular areas of a beach. I go to the quiet scarcer areas if possible. When planning a trip or getaway you will want to ensure that you're not going to a place that is a popular tourist trap. You won't go to see a blockbuster movie the weekend it opens, but wait a couple of weeks when the immediate crowds die down. These are some of the basic examples of how you can organize and conduct your life in ways that will lessen the input of harsh energies from people around you.

There are phobias that are beyond being a natural sensitive and compassionate human soul. All phobias are a fear of something pertaining to whatever that phobia is. Fear itself is not based in reality. You are giving the fear power and control over you. Fear is created and conjured up in the mind. Your mind draws up conclusions that it's afraid of something that the average person doesn't see or comprehend. It can take a lifetime to manage the fear. Sometimes it will require the specialties of a therapist or hypnotherapist to dig into the real truth of the issue causing this fear. Often the fear is related to something from childhood or a specific traumatic experience that has stayed lodged into one's mind. It can be more than one traumatic experience say if that person was abused in any way growing up. It's been so long since the negative experience happened that the soul is unaware that they've learned this fear from something that happened so long ago.

If someone is raped by a very large man, it is not unusual for that person to suddenly develop a new fear that entails finding that their heart races whenever they run into a large man or any man for that matter. Even though the large man they are running into is perfectly harmless, a fight or flight fear response is triggered in the brain that equates all large men to be a threat, when this is not always true. A woman was telling me that a dog she adopted from the shelter is happy and go lucky, but whenever it encounters a man, the dog's ears flip back, tail drops and it whimpers and hides. The woman believed that the dog may have been previously abused by a male figure and therefore equates all men to be a threat. She's had the dog for years and the dog still reacts in this way.

Conquering the fear requires that you put in the daily work to overcome what is causing the fear. It requires a thorough evaluation process to go back into time to find out what triggered the fear response. You must then take daily action steps in working on overcoming the fears. It is more or less about re-training the mind. The mind is a powerful thing. It can manifest on a whim simply with its thoughts. Thoughts produce circumstances, therefore, watching your thoughts and working on re-training your mind on how it perceives things is the way to overcome phobias.

My agoraphobia still exists, but it's not as bad as it was growing up. Improvement has been made, but I'm still not going to throw myself into crowds for no reason. This isn't due completely to the agoraphobia, but being an energetic psychic sponge means you absorb these intense energies and find them to be interfering on your equilibrium. My aura and soul around my body needs space and suffocates in massive crowds. It's like a fish out of water unable to function. This is beyond what was learned growing up in a human life. It was already in the DNA of that human soul when they entered this life. The DNA is the makeup that was engrained in that soul far beyond incarnating into a human life. The DNA is present in the soul at its conception.

Chapter Eight

The Love and
Relationship Life for a
Wise One and the
Knights Paladin

If Wise Ones are natural born teachers, leaders, communicators, motivators and military sergeants, then what do you think you're going to get in a love relationship with someone like that? Many Wise Ones find they end up in relationships with a soul mate that might be a student type subconsciously wanting to learn or gain knowledge from them or that person is an evolving soul. This is regardless of their age. A Wise One can be 30 years old and in a relationship with a student who is 40 years old. It comes with the territory that when you're in a relationship with a Wise One, you're involved with a know it all. The great love partner for a Wise One is the soul mate who doesn't allow the Wise One's know-it-all nature to be a problem for them. It is not seen as a negative trait. On the flip side, the Wise One should be mindful and aware when they are moving into a Counselor or Coach role when communicating with their soul mate partner about something that doesn't require that tone. Wise Ones also match up well with other leaders and those diving into philosophical and spiritual pursuits.

They are incredibly loyal, trustworthy and dedicated in a relationship. These are the same noble traits you would find in a Knight in Shining Armor. Knights throughout the ages were incarnated from the Realm of the Wise Ones, but many of them were half-breed Wise Ones who had fallen into what is called the Realm of the Knights Paladin. A Knight Paladin in a human life is half Wise One and half Incarnated Angel. These are angels that inhabit the Wise One form in the Wise One Realm. They have an even mix of the darker strength of the Wise One and the compassionate giving soul of the Incarnated Angel. Knight Paladin's make excellent mates for either the Wise One or Incarnated Angel since they have an understanding and connection to both worlds. Knight Paladin's are all about order and honor, but they are also giving and protecting. They tend to be muscular or have strong athletic builds. They may also be male or female in human form. They stand at attention and have the label of being the strong, silent type. Think of the image of the actors, Daniel Craig or Matthew McConaughey. The actresses would be someone like Angela Bassett or Jodie Foster.

Knight Paladin's are the guys you would find in the military, and working as CIA or FBI agents, security guards or as law enforcement officers. They're usually quieter than the full-blooded Wise One who lectures in long windedness via phone, email, video, or a stage audience platform. The athletic builds of the Knight Paladin is due to the Wise One influence. Many Wise Ones are big on physical fitness, nutrition and other forms of body improvement. These are the ones that spend their lifetime in the outdoors taking care of their mind, body and soul. They know the importance of keeping their bodies as strong and healthy as possible. This gives them more energy and focus to accomplish their goals. If a Wise One resorts to addictive behaviors, they will somehow balance that out with a workout regimen that eventually dominates and wipes out the addictive behavior.

Wise Ones make top-notch mates for those in the Incarnated Elemental Realms. In fact, many Wise Ones tend to be in relationships with those from the Elemental realm. Some of these include blended elementals and some not. It's a case of opposites attract, but they both have that fighting nature as a common denominator and understanding. When a Wise One and Incarnated Elemental get in a relationship, it is instant camaraderie with an, "us against the world" view. They both have strengths that the other lacks and it meets effortlessly. They make a beeline to one another like magnets when they cross paths. It's usually the Incarnated Elementals who makes the first move otherwise the deal will never be sealed, but the Wise One meets more than half way.

Both of the Spirit Worlds of the Wise Ones and the Incarnated Elementals overlap and blend in with one another. It's no surprise that their relationship works well together because they already inhabit the same place on the other side! This was described in the beginning of this book. They also overlap in the human Earth world. Back in ancient history, they would be out in nature together worshipping and summoning the spirit energy under the planetary alignments of the heavens. They both love being outdoors in nature and would likely get a place together in such a locale. Incidentally, the Wise One tends to be in relationships with those younger, while the Incarnated Elementals seem to be in relationships with those that are older. This is not always the case of course, but generally speaking there is that pattern.

A relationship between a Wise One and Incarnated Elemental has its challenges to a degree as all relationships do. There is that "opposites attract" factor going on between them. Some days lead them to repel each other or the connection becomes tempestuous due to their egos and passionate natures. Their instant compatibility soon draws them back together. Elementals can be a little flip floppy where they are here, there and everywhere. Some find this confusion frustrating when it has to do with a serious relationship. However, the Elementals soon dart right back around to the Wise One again. This is interesting since in the Realms, the Elementals fly and move about all over the place. They mingle and fly in with the Wise One, then dart out in another direction before re-surfacing again next to them. When the Wise One needs an army, they bring the Elemental on board who is a tough and willing soldier.

Elementals love to be carefree and roaming. They need space and freedom preferably in the great outdoors. This freedom does not have anything to do with what a human soul would consider to be cheating. Suddenly they come back circling the Wise One demanding their attention. A Wise One offers the stability they crave, while the Elementals soften the Wise Ones rigidness. They help the Wise One to lighten up and have some fun once in awhile! There is everlasting loyalty between the Wise One and an Incarnated Elemental. This works in a long-term relationship marriage or commitment. They both fight important causes that are connected to humanity in some way. The Wise One organizes the home base ensuring the bills are paid even if they both contribute to the bills. While the Elementals spruce up the interior decorating and landscaping of the property. An Incarnated Elemental may want to have animals for pets. It's as if the animals are there babies. This doesn't always bother the Wise One since it gives them alone time to do their extracurricular activities while the Elemental is off and running with the dogs outside.

Wise Ones and Elementals are accustomed to living in the denser atmospheres such as Earth. Where there is density, there is also intensity! They both have the larger egos of all the realms. Where there is ego, there is going to be some intensity and fiery energy. They are also the warriors and fighter spirits on the other side. This is an additional element that adds to the intensity and fiery energy in their connection.

Wise Ones have a strong presence that is difficult to penetrate. Love is no exception causing potential suitors to find the Wise One too challenging to get involved with. The exceptions are the Elementals who rise to the challenge as they have the similar difficult nature. The right soul mate suitor will not stop until they nab the Wise One. The Wise One takes notice and adores the persistence the suitor put into getting to know them. Those who give up pretty quickly are added to a long list of "no name" suspects that the Wise One has no affinity towards. They abhor human souls that are unable to put in any kind of work or fight, since the Wise One is all about the hard work in all aspects of their life.

The Wise Ones are not sensitive in the way an Incarnated Angel might be. Incarnated Angels feel hurt and saddened when slighted. They will protest that they don't understand how someone could be cruel to them. They will spend their nights in tears unable to sleep trying to get over being slighted. Whereas, when a Wise One is slighted in a love relationship, they rise to anger and sometimes vengeance! They may at first lie awake at night feeling defeated and hurt that a suitor walked out on them or cheated. The tears that a Wise One sheds soon grow to cold icicles. This fuels the upsurge of a powerful Phoenix rising from the ashes. A Wise One can be dangerous when slighted, so it's best to know what you're getting involved with beforehand. They are apt to lash out when wronged by someone regardless of who it is. They might come off eerily polite, but be warned they are indeed plotting something beyond what can be understood.

Despite the dark toughness of the Wise One nature, they are softies when it comes to romantic relationships. This is why some partake in divination tools, spells and magic. They have a romantic heart when with the right person and will do anything possible to manifest and conjure that up. Think of the Knight image previously described. When the Wise One has the right partner who opens up their heart, there is no telling what they and their partner can accomplish together. The Wise One needs to beware of getting stuck in a loveless relationship or with someone who is battling addiction issues. This will sink the heart of the Wise One causing them to delay or even stop them from working on their purpose. This is why it is important that the Wise One requests that Heaven send them a high vibrational soul who will be loving, supportive and a great companion who is independent and has their own life. Wise Ones may be difficult to approach, but the right one won't give up or lose interest in the chase. This shows that the suitor's intentions are true.

Star People make best friendships with a Wise One. This is also a great match to start up a successful company together. They're both hardworking and offer crucial expertise that the other might not see. In a romantic love relationship is where the frictions between a Star Person and Wise One may reside. The Wise One can function in a relationship with a Star Person, but the Wise Ones are passionate oriented and the Star Person can get by without resorting to any of that intensity. It's this intensity that the Wise One craves in a hot love relationship.

The Wise One and Star Person are disciplined when it comes to hard work. The problem is when in a love relationship together, they may both fall into the space of hard work and forget about the romance. The Wise One will notice this imbalance fairly quickly and will grow agitated when they discover that months have gone by and the Star Person has yet to show affection. The Wise One may shrivel up in a love relationship with a Star Person. Wise Ones need daily physical expressions of love since Wise Ones are all about the physical in general.

When the Wise One is heated and in ego, the Star Person is unaffected or unfazed by it. Those from the Star Person Realm tend to be void of expressing any major emotion. They have a detached monotone voice when cutting right to the heart of the matter. This is why a Star Person could handle the Wise One nature in a business setting with ease. When the Wise One is pacing and having a tantrum about something not being done, the Star Person barely rolls their eyes and may utter some sentence of advice. "How about if we do it this way?" The Wise One will stop the pacing and narrow their eyes almost judging them, but then say, "You're right. We need to....."

One of my friends is a Star Person. Everything he says somehow leads to aliens and extraterrestrials. He always seems to weave it into his sentences somehow here and there. I mentioned this to him once and he denied it and asked, "When do I do that?" I said, "Five minutes ago. You said, "I really love my car. It's like a gigantic spaceship. Ford is really coming together and they're going intergalactic with the controls." Suddenly before I could finish my sentence he busted out laughing realizing it was true. He says, "Oh wow, you're right, I didn't realize I do that!"

He made an observation that actress Sandra Bullock is a Star Person. This is specifically her choice to do the film, *Gravity*. I pointed out that this was interesting. The movie *Gravity* was pretty much solely her throughout most of the film. It was her in a space pod floating around. I said, "Why would an actress of her caliber choose to do that? Because Sandra Bullock the person and not the actress likely feels comfortable in a space environment." Some of her other roles allude to psychic phenomena such as, "Premonition" or "Practical Magic". There was the movie, "Speed", where she's in control of a bus as if it were a spaceship for most of the movie. Her choice to do, "The Blind Side", shows the Star Person's influence in playing a character that has the compassion in helping someone in need. Star People in films love to entertain through comedy release as she has done in movies like, "Miss Congeniality", "The Proposal", and "The Heat".

Incarnated Cherubs may sometimes be too much for a Wise One's equilibrium. It's too much energy being darted at them. Wise Ones need calm and nature much like the Elementals. Cherubs are fun loving and great in small doses for the Wise One, but when a Wise One and Cherub are sitting next to one another, the differences are obvious.

Incarnated Cherubs are half Incarnated Angel and half Star Person. The Star person aspect gives them that "get up and go" to start a business. I know one Cherub who runs her own Esthetician business and loves everything clothes, fashion, pampering, restaurants, beauty, waxing and facials. This is right on target with the purpose of an Incarnated Cherub who enjoys working with people. A Cherub will shrivel up without human sociable contact. They always need to have the best and will point it out if it doesn't appear to be that way. They always seem to be in a relationship and are not considered shy. They immediately light up with all smiles when someone walks in the door or room. The Cherub will start peppering them with questions. They can be very loud and chatty. You can hear a Cherub when they've arrived. They love to lavish themselves and others with gifts. The cuter the gifts, the better! The giving nature is right on par with an Incarnated Cherub. If they could have a credit card that never maxes out, then they would be in *real* Heaven. An Incarnated Cherub puts on elaborate dinners with people. They usually grow angry or depressed when they fear a love partner is not being devoted and giving them all of their time.

Wise Ones are the opposite in demeanor. They can be a little uptight if a stranger approaches them abundantly animated and chatty. The condescending brick wall flies up around them when someone comes at them with questions they have no intention of answering.

Incarnated Angels want to talk about their feelings and emotions for hours. If you get them on the phone, you may never get off with them. They feel right at home opening up with someone. This is different than the long windedness of a Wise One. The long windedness of the Incarnated Angel is when they're talking about how someone has hurt them. They will go over the horrid treatment by a lover for eons. Whereas the Wise One is long winded in their advice and guidance. They too will go over what someone did in great detail, but they don't do it from a place of being a victim. It's done more in a way of dissecting their opponent's move and how they will react to it. This is in the same way an army soldier will strategize.

One of the negatives that can happen for a Wise One in a relationship with an Incarnated Angel is that the Incarnated Angel wants to talk endlessly about their daily problems. This will grow wearing on the Wise One who demands occasional silence. They are turned off by the toxicity that comes in the form of daily complaints. They can only listen to the same complaints enough times from someone who feels constantly mistreated by the world before they snap. Wise Ones demand that others improve themselves. If a soul chooses to remain stagnant refusing to take action steps to improve a situation, then the Wise One grows irritated. You can see how these two may feel somewhat of an understanding of one another and wanting to communicate, yet the feeling and intention behind the communication is quite different.

Sometimes an Incarnated Angel may attach themselves to a Wise One too tightly enjoying the stability and security the Wise One gives off. The Wise One finds they have to loosen the grip a little bit when it starts to feel too co-dependent. The Wise Ones love and appreciate the Incarnated Angels heart. They almost want to protect them from the cruelty that seems to be inflicted upon the angel on a regular basis. At the same time, the Wise One has a sacred space around them where they do not want lower energies around them full time. Lower energies can come in the form of martyrdom and daily complaints. The Incarnated Angel doesn't intend to be in that space, but they feel so low from the horrid and hurtful treatment by someone that they cannot help it.

Incarnated Angels have a tendency to end up in co-dependent relationships or feeling like they can save the troubled, dysfunctional person they are in a relationship with. I've counseled some who had moved into committed relationships with these co-dependent connections, and then complained during that relationship. I'll ask, "...but, weren't they like this before you guys got married or got into a committed relationship?" There will be a long pause of silence then a meek response. "Yes, but I thought..." I'll interrupt, "You thought he'd suddenly become a different person once you were married? Marriage doesn't make a troubled connection better. In fact, it blows those eccentricities out into the open even more!"

Those from the various Realms sometimes find they get into relationships with souls who are also from a specific Realm. This is not always the case. They can be called into a relationship with someone who is not from a Realm and instead might be a toxic partner. Someone from a Realm can be toxic, but this toxicity fades to a good degree when they realize their calling and purpose. Eventually the person from a Realm evolves out of their toxic behavior. There may be signs that they have evolved and or are evolving over time.

Can a Wise One be corrupted on Earth? They can be difficult, hotheaded and extra sure of themselves that their ego sometimes gets away with them from time to time. It is not common for a Wise One to be corrupted in a human body for long. They will usually transform at some point in their life onto the right path before their human death. The Wise One's energy is so great that it's almost impossible to not have that grand wake-up call that sets them down on their life purpose.

My friendships are all across the board with those from all realms. They are my soul brothers, sisters and cousins from another realm. I tend to get along with a variety of different personalities even though strangely enough I wouldn't be able to necessarily put them all in the same room together and hope they'll hit it off. There are other astrological influences on top of the Realm influences that make the union between two people an interesting cocktail that can attract or repel them from each other. It's important to consider all factors that make up the totality of one person.

Wise Ones or those in other Realms do not always get involved in love relationships with one another. Sometimes they get involved with those who are new human souls to bring enlightenment or for a specific purpose in enabling that person's soul growth. Usually when someone from a Realm gets involved with a new soul, there is going to be trouble in that relationship. It's sometimes like dealing with a child. Wise Ones are used to being in the teacher role or dominating role even if it's not in their profession. They innately seem to get in relationships with those who are a new soul, younger soul, or a soul open to gain knowledge. This is not always the case, but it is for the most part.

Here is an example of a Wise One and Incarnated Elemental mix. Dan is in his sixties and Bonnie is in her fifties. Dan is a serious and brooding Wise One. He's a world traveler, professor and doctor who speaks several languages. He doesn't talk to you unless you approach him. When you do, get ready to sit back as he expounds for an hour on a question you've asked him. He's always seen with a glass of wine and holding a book under his arm to gain additional knowledge and research. His wife Bonnie is an Incarnated Elemental who rolls her eyes behind him when he's droning on. She's giving and upbeat. As discussed, Dan falls into the older Wise One with his younger Incarnated Elemental mate, Bonnie. Bonnie rallies the neighborhood together to have days where they clean up the beach, or other important environmental causes. Like all Elementals and some Wise Ones, Bonnie made a joke on one beach cleanup day. An empty bottle of liquor, cigarettes and box of condoms was discovered together in a pile. She used her protective gloves to pick the items up and throw them in the trash bag. As she did this, she made an announcement of what she was picking up, then finished it off with a joke. "We're going out to party!" She giggled waving the stuff in the air. Dan and Bonnie will be on an airplane together and she's reading People Magazine about celebrity's lives, while he's working on math problems for fun.

How about a Wise One in another relationship with another Wise One? Here you will find two souls who are immediately on the same telepathic wave length able to know the other's needs. If there is any friction that arises it's merely that you've got two long winded know it all's in a relationship together. Yet, Wise Ones who are fighting the same causes together, with the same beliefs and values while facing the same direction will not see this as a negative. It is comforting to know that someone understands them more than anyone else. It is like being in a strong army of two conquering the world and everything in it as a team. Nothing will slip through the cracks with this duo!

The Wise Ones are the love mates who whip out the charts, graphs and power point presentations to lay out the nature of their relationship. Not everyone wants to be lectured and forced to study a timeline of events in a graph that includes when you upset the Wise One in a managerial presentation! Their minds work in high level ways that it might sometimes feel as if you're married to an executive at a corporation. This would be no surprise considering that Wise Ones are out in the world running successful enterprises. Love, loyalty, security and passion intertwine this ferocious power couple.

Are you in a relationship with a Wise One and planning a vacation together? The Wise One is the mate who breaks down all of the possible choices on where to go and where to stay to the point of being difficult to please. The pros and cons are all listed out as they pour over the details with you for weeks before the trip. By this point, you're so worn out from the decision making process that you'll accept going anywhere as long as you can relax and not listen to any additional choices and lists! The Wise One means well, but is such a perfectionist who wants to ensure everyone is having a good time. They enjoy including their mate in the decision making process as it makes them feel as if they're working as part of a team. You're in it together and care about every factor of the relationship. Your opinion in the relationship matters to them despite their tendency to talk down or at someone without realizing it.

Chapter Nine

Planetary Talk

Being a Wise One is more than appearing serious and dark. Wise Ones are also quite charming, seductive and alluring to those around them. They're a wealth of information and are easily right on the mark. Sometimes the information they relay can fly right over other people's heads. It's almost too much information for others to soak in at times. The hyper-technological age has dominated much of the world's influence to a series of sound bites. This dumb downs the public rather than educates them. The mind has the capacity to soak up a vast reservoir of knowledge and yet the mass majority has been trained to allow minimal input before it collapses. The Wise Ones working in modern day times can be challenging, but this doesn't detour them. It is in their nature and part of their design to distribute the information regardless if anyone sees or understands it.

Wise Ones have been known to be some of history's great astrologers. This isn't the horoscope section that you read in the back of a trashy magazine.

This is the intricate study of the positions of the planets in space. It's studying how they move and to what degree they move. They are able to accurately assess how the planets position affects the energy within a human soul. They can tell how the planet positions affect the entire globe as a whole. Human souls who incarnated from the Realm of the Wise One have been responsible for bringing our discovery of these planets to the masses. They have incarnated over the course of history to bring in the art of astrology while continuing to expand and improve on it. On the other side, the Wise Ones are naturally gifted astrologers who have been studying the positions and makings of the planets in all dimensions for all lifetimes. The Wise One looks up towards the sky and their heightened vision and mind immediately computes data knowing exactly where the planet is and how it will affect someone's behavior. It is not surprising to find that most of Earth's astrologers and astronomers, including the Mayans and Vedic Astrologers are indeed from the Realm of the Wise Ones.

Astrology was considered a science centuries ago. In today's jaded modern world, the Astrology name has been a little tainted due to the rise in amateurs teaching others about the Sun Sign and horoscopes, but nothing else. These are the ones that believe that if someone has their sun sign in a particular sign, then they must be a certain way. This is untrue as one's Sun Sign is only the beginning of building the structure that makes up that individual.

For example, two people have their Sun Sign in Capricorn, but one is a serious, quiet person, while the other is on the jolly side always smiling. When you delve deeper into that person's chart to examine where this nature in their personality is coming from, you will discover where the culprit lies. Perhaps one of the Capricorns has their Rising sign in Taurus, while the other has their Rising in Gemini. The one that has the Gemini rising is most likely the happy go lucky type of Capricorn, while the other one with the Taurus rising is more on the quiet, serious side. Knowing this information is helpful when looking at relationship compatibility. This is an important question that others want to know when it comes to love. I know a Sun in Cancer person who has been in a long-term successful love relationship with a Sun in Sagittarius person. If you were to just look at their Sun Signs, you would automatically say they're incompatible. However, if you delved deeper into their charts you would discover that the other elements in their chart are what have brought them together and kept them there.

Wise Ones tend to be affected by the Mercury Retrograde transit more than any other transit. The planet Mercury rules all things related to Communication and Transportation. Three times a year, the planet moves retrograde for three weeks affecting the energy on the planet in terms of communication and transportation. Wise Ones are natural communicators regardless if their means is through writing, speaking, teaching or leading. This is all in the realms of communication. When Mercury moves retrograde, the energy in the Wise One slows down. This may be a bit of a hindrance because they're used to operating on high energy whether physically or mentally. This doesn't matter because once Mercury starts to move retrograde, that all shifts within them.

For me, I can feel the energy within me slowing down. This starts building about a week before Mercury actually goes retrograde. I grow quieter and more distant than usual, which is nice for some others. If I don't know when the transit is happening or haven't looked it up, I can sense it. I'll say out of the blue, "Mercury is about to go retrograde." Whichever friend I'm with will say, "How do you know?" I'll say, "Because I can feel it."

My friend and I will then look up when the next Mercury Retrograde is only to discover were smack dab in the shadow of the Retrograde. The plus is the transit makes me more introspective and great ideas that were dormant rise to the surface. The Mercury Retrograde transit has an added benefit for writers, communicators and artists as it leads to inspiration and ideas.

The planets transits have some measure of an effect on how souls act out. Regardless of any planetary activity that occurs on a regular basis, the fighting and projecting of fears and anger from human souls is all year long. A planet's transit merely heightens or lessons that energy depending on its movement in the Heavens. This is much like how the Moon affects the ocean tides. The energy pull is the same with how the planets align with one another. Planets do not break people up, but they will break up those who were already having challenges to begin with. The planets just show them the way. When you have an understanding of how the planetary transits affect human behavior, then you can use that to your advantage when making major decisions in your life.

The outer planets such as Uranus, Neptune and Pluto affect global and social issues. This is seen when there is a rise in culture or world wars and accidents. The planet Uranus is what may cause abrupt changes as it rarely plays by the rules. The Pluto Retrograde heightens destructive tendencies. The outer planets usually move retrograde once a year and for most of the year. They don't necessarily play a huge a part on the day-to-day grind that the inner planets might. They tend to shake up long-term changes whether internally or externally. The inner planets like Mercury, Venus and Mars tend to have an effect on the day-to-day lives of human souls. Jupiter and Saturn are the center planets that effect both interpersonal and global issues.

Sadly the fighting and antagonism that are currently going on around the world will continue for years to come as long as human souls are starving for power and domination. When this many souls are disconnected to what's outside of themselves, then you will have never-ending chaos. The headlines show that there is no inner peace, but only anger and fear. It's been this way since human conception here on Earth. Although there have been positive changes over the course of history, it doesn't move as fast as it would if every human soul remained in their natural state. Be the example of one who is evolving and aware. Allow the goodness that exists within you to rub off on one another. Let it get passed around the globe instead of the nasty ego energy. To say things are changing as a collective is a positive way to look at the state of things. The reality is if human souls were changing much more rapidly, then I and the others from the various Realms would not have had to come here in historical numbers to enact and contribute positive changes for humanity and Earth.

Chapter Ten

Wiccans, Witches, Wizards, Mediums and Sorcerers

Wise Ones are also Wiccans, Witches, Wizards and Sorcerers. The Wise Ones are associated with magic on the other side so it's no surprise that as human souls they have some degree of knowledge with it, even if they are not practicing Wicca. The Wise One can be part of a Catholic Parish and still be versed or open minded to the ways of how magic and manifestation works. Even if they are not partaking in magic, it's likely a subject that attracts and fascinates them. This applies to all Wise Ones. They might be a teacher or professor who doesn't believe in an afterlife, yet others may note the many principles they enforce that are aligned with magic and manifestation.

Wise Ones on the other side disappear and evaporate into a ray of light when they move about. They can move from one place to the next in the blink of an eye. This coincides with the magic spell power we see in mythological pieces surrounding the Wizard who disappears in a puff of smoke. There is the Warlock who throws his dark black cloak around him and vanishes into the darkness of the woods. How about the Hunter who swings from tree to tree at the speed of light? He moves so quickly that it looks as if he's disappeared, but rather he has blended into the environment like an animal stalking his prey. Because of the hunting nature of the Wise One, it's also not uncommon for Wise Ones on Earth to find themselves in jobs or careers that allow them to use these hunting gifts. This can be in some of our history's great detectives to a top-notch research specialist in any field. If the fictional character Sherlock Holmes were indeed real, he would be a Wise One.

Throughout the course of my life, I've had other employers comment at how I could track down the answer to most anything. Some had referred to me as a skilled research investigator or having the voice of a radio host in communications. I have had no Earth training to be one. The Wise Ones have the gift of knowing. Because of this, nothing eludes them and they know when someone is lying even if they do not call them out on it. They most often know someone's every move before that person has made it.

Wise Ones have the gift of prophecy and a major interest in the occult and the science of astrology such as Wise One, Nostradamus. He was also a Scientist, Astrologer and Doctor with an analytical and medical background. Nostradamus, like other Wise Ones, was also considered a great healer, prophet and clairvoyant. All those human souls who have incarnated from any Realm have one thing in common and that is they make awesome healers in some way. Some may not even choose the healing profession, but somewhere in their nature the healing aspects that are part of their natural gifts do sneak out. Wise Ones tend to be of the Sage variety. They love working with magic, dark arts, the Tarot as well as other forms of ancient mysticism. Although they are basically good-natured, there is that dark side that often takes over and shows itself. They are the High Priests and High Priestesses that utilize divination tools such as the Tarot, Voodoo dolls, Runes, Pendulums, Psychic Boards, Crystal Balls, Automatic Writing and Angel cards. Some do not use any divination tool and allow the information to flow through their soul. You'll find some of these Wise Ones living in New Orleans practicing the magic arts day after day. Wise Ones would come in the form of the fictional characters played by Jessica Lange and Angela Bassett in "American Horror Story: The Coven".

Wise Ones are natural channelers and Mediums. Even if they do not practice that kind of work, those gifts and traits exist within them. One notable Wise One in history is the mysticist, Edgar Cayce, who brought some of the spiritual and enlightenment craft to light. He spoke about Atlantis and the Akashic Records. He delivered his messages and information in books as an author. This is the perfect way for a Wise One to express their interests. They can be as longwinded as they like in a book, while talking about and teaching the subjects they enjoy. The Wise Ones also practiced and brought Shamanism to the planet. This has been big with the super gifted Wise One Native Americans or American Indians. They revel in channeling, altered states of consciousness, trances and rituals. North America was a spiritual open land before the outside settlers took over pushing the American Indians out of the way. They forced a puritanical, superstitious, religious belief system on the people and its land. This along with materialistic drive, domination and ego lowered the energy vibration of the North American territory.

Joan of Arc is a soul from the Realm of the Wise One. She was also highly prophetic and a soldier who went at it alone. In that sentence we hit three basic Wise One traits. They are *in tune, strong fighters,* who work *independently.* Wise Ones have no problem going it alone, as they are independent personified. They need to be in control and generally rise to a leadership role in the areas that interest them. Joan of Arc was burned at the stake in the 19th century when she was 19 years old. She was considered guilty of witchcraft. She was never a witch in the way that the world believed a witch to be. If you had views that were advanced and misunderstood, or you claimed to hear, see, feel and know the heavenly messages being relayed to you by God, angels, spirit guides, saints or archangels, then you were considered a witch. This was regardless of you being male or female. When one thinks of a witch in modern day society, they picture the woman that looks to be 500 years old with a green face, cape, pointy hat and a broom. The real witches that exist look like everybody else.

Joan of Arc had clairvoyant visions passed onto her by God, Saint Michael the Archangel, Saint Margaret and Saint Catherine to help save France from being taken over by the English. She was a Wise One on the other side before entering that lifetime with this sole purpose. She led an army and went to battle in order to accomplish this. She helped France regain control, but was captured by the English and burned for her clairvoyant visions. Her crime was witchcraft. They did not believe that God would tell her to dress up like a man and go into battle. This is evil! Of course, God did instruct her to do just that. We have progressed over the centuries that it is no longer unusual for a woman to have this kind of control. There are still some third world countries that force women to take a back seat. They might be slow to evolve as souls, but for the most part it is no longer considered strange for a woman to dress up as a man and head into battle.

France did not step in when Joan was captured even though she assisted Charles VII to obtain the throne as King of France at that time. Almost 500 years later the Catholic Church finally realized that Joan was wrongly executed. They made her a Saint under the eyes of the Church. It's not uncommon for some Wise Ones to evolve into Saints or Ascended Masters. Saints and Ascended Masters are *all knowing* teachers so naturally they are also from the Realm of the Wise One.

I've known I was a Wise One for a good chunk of my life, although I did not equate a title to it such as "Wise One". I did not flinch when a well-known Wise One Medium friend had uttered it during one of our conversations. She said, "You and I used to mix with magic and potions on the other side. You + me = psychic twins." I said, "I know. We are magical magicians on the other side with our spells and potions."

Spell Work

On Earth, the Wise One that operates as a Witch or Warlock will look to the moon and planetary phases when wanting to cast a spell efficiently. This is aligned with those who excel at astrology and astronomy. Spell work is seen as negative, dark and black in some circles. Those who believe this have been watching too many Hollywood movies! Or they've latched onto a false idea taken from biblical text that it's evil, when that is not the case. If a passage aligns itself with superstitions, then this is a clue that it is not of God. God does not instill fear into someone. Only the ego of a human soul would do that. Deciphering what is real and what is fiction is simple to detect in that respect. When you are really in tune with God, you would know what he forbids. If you have caused, 'hurt, harm or hate', then you have defied God. This is God in any manner that you know God to be.

Spell casting is manipulating energy. You are doing this everyday through your actions and words regardless if you know anything about spell casting or not. If everyone is made up of energy, then they have the power to bend it to however they choose. When you're in a great mood, you notice that everyone around you is the same. When you're in a bad mood, you discover that one negative thing after another starts to happen.

As a Wise One, I have been working with magic energy throughout all of my lifetimes. It comes to me naturally when I'm home on the other side. This energy light can be seen for miles over there. While here, the Earth's atmosphere is too compressed and heavy. I can still draw up this energy from within my soul, gathering it up like a farmer gathers crops. I pull it out of my soul with my hands carrying it, then I take that energy light and place it between my hands, then watch it expand. This magical spirit force grows and clairvoyantly looks much like a supernova at full capacity. For that matter, it can be dangerous if I'm riled up and toss it out into the universe like a baseball - which I have done in the past specifically in the spirit world. Tossing it out upwards for fun it's seen blasting apart in the Heavens above in a brilliant light colored show.

There are the love spells, revenge spells, bring my ex back spells. This frightens those not familiar with how spells work. Spells are energy that can be manipulated, or directed. It depends on the power of the spell caster as to how potent the energy is going to be. An experienced spell caster knows how to shield themselves so that the energy doesn't hit them. There is a cause and effect to spells.

A spell caster cannot force an ex suitor to come back to somebody. What they can do is manipulate the magic energy that prompts you to seem more attractive to that other person. How that other person responds to it is left up to that person's free will choice. They can deny the intensity out of not understanding why they're more attracted than usual or they can move with it. This magic energy can be one that is designed to boost your self-confidence or self-love. By doing that, you find yourself displaying a burst of positive energy, optimism and confidence. These are qualities you radiate after the spell is cast. It's qualities that attract in positive circumstances and people, including a love interest.

For example, someone who has a same sex attraction cannot have a spell cast to have someone who is not attracted to the same sex want them. If one were to do a test to see what would happen, the straight person might be intrigued or drawn towards the person who is gay. It would be an intense friendship they were feeling. You cannot force or make someone who isn't attracted to a specific gender fall head over heels for them. I don't know of any particular cases where this has happened, but I'm illustrating through this scenario on how a spell will likely not work.

Spell energy fades and so will the love if that person isn't already enamored by you. How long spell energy lasts is debatable, but typically anywhere from say one month up to a year. The closer to the year mark you get the more that energy has dissolved over the course of that period.

Since the Wise Ones manifest easily and produce magic energy just as effortlessly, they must be careful with how they're directing energy. Wise Ones can easily and sometimes unknowingly cause harm to other people just by the sheer power of their thoughts and intentions. They know and have a deep understanding of manifestation that it's sometimes uncontrollable. In the Spirit Realm, the manifestation magic capabilities flow through their light with the blink of one eye. Look to the image of the Wise One, Merlin to gain an idea of the Wizard who manifests on a whim using his magical spell casting gifts.

Abundance

It's true that having the great relationship, career, home and car won't necessarily make you happy, but you may likely be happier. It's a human need to desire the basic necessities of life. However, a great many people who obtain these things still protest to not feeling happy and satisfied afterwards. I run in many circles that include those who are obscenely wealthy, as well as friends and acquaintances that are well known publicly due to my previous work in the entertainment business. I can tell you their problems are not any less important than anybody else's. They have money, a great career and popularity, sure, but they still have internal personal issues they are battling that have to be addressed. They have endless flowing money and are not completely content. This is because true happiness comes from within. You start there and then work your way externally. When you are experiencing joy and contentment inside, then the other needs manifest more quickly.

The fine print needs to be stated because often in some spiritual contexts it is taught that happiness comes from within and that craving a great relationship or career will not make you happy. If you are always feeling miserable and then you obtain the great career, it may still leave you feeling empty, but it could possibly offer you added fulfillment that will elevate your vibration. If you're miserable, it is highly unlikely you would attract and obtain a great relationship or career to begin with anyway. A wonderful fulfilling love relationship will enhance your life that is already enhanced. Bottom line is find that space within you that helps you to feel satisfied now, and then the rest will follow. The abundance of wealth, love and home will be an added bonus that enriches your life even more. You are then able to put more focus on others, help those in need, and change things that need shifting in this world. When you are lavished in abundance, you are in a brighter mind space to focus on your life purpose without the added need of personal worries like paying your bills or finding a love relationship.

The key to abundance is feeling it before you see it. You feel it by believing it. It's in the way that you think and function. You can get there by saying affirmations to yourself daily until its part of your life and part of your soul. I am exhilarated. I am love. I am joy. I am in a place of perfect contentment. All my needs are met. All my desires are met. I sit back in awe at the wonders around me. I am taken care of in all ways. I have no needs because what I require as a human soul flows to me effortlessly. Abundance flows to me like water. I don't need it, but it is there and keeps on coming. I feel bliss. I am uplifted. I am always laughing. I am always seeing the humor around me. What I need is here with me now. I sit in peace and notice the abundance and love flow to me and around me like a spinning wheel. The more content I am, then the more the abundance flows. When I am resistant I am not there. When I am emotional I am not there. When I stand strong in confidence I am there. When I am sure of myself I am there. When I give love I am there. When I allow myself to receive love I am there. When I have compassion I am there.

These are examples of the thoughts that need to dominate your less than stellar thoughts in order to bring more abundance to you.

Let's say you were laid off from your job and you want to pursue the career of your dreams in opening up an art gallery. You know this will cost at least twenty grand in a good area. The devastation of being laid off from one's job depending on the scenario can be a blessing in disguise. It's a great sign to take you out of your comfort zone. It's understood about the ramifications that come out of being laid off or leaving a job in any form. The angels also understand that as human souls we have to survive, we have groceries to pick up and we have bills to pay. The flip side is that it's almost a blessing in disguise giving you the freedom to choose what you are going to do next. Going after work that is your passion takes some orchestrating and maneuvering.

When I was sixteen I knew I would be writing books. I knew that I wouldn't start writing books out of the gate. I decided to first look for a job where I could incorporate creativity, writing and storytelling. The entertainment business came to mind and I went on a huge hunt and fight to get in. When I turned twenty-three years old, I was hired by one of the top box office actresses at the time to read scripts and write coverage on it for her production company. It had the best of all worlds I was looking for to incorporate writing in some way. I was doing some writing work while getting paid. This led to the next thing and all great things came down from that.

If you wanted to open your art gallery, then consider pursuing obtaining a job in an art gallery. You're not going to start your own studio tomorrow, but perhaps look for work that is somehow connected to that world and genre so that you're inside. Accepting work as an assistant in an art gallery puts you in the arena of your interest. Be the receptionist if it gets you into that world. Take whatever work position you need to take that gets you in the door of the genre that is your interest and the rest will follow.

We're all teachers and have much to learn from one another. Everyone is important. Everyone has the ability to communicate with Heaven, God, Archangels, Saints and Angels and so on. No one is more special than anybody else in that regard. Wise Ones help others improve themselves and their life by having a crystal clear communication with the other side. The main messages are of joy, peace and happiness. Prepare to make leaps of change that you desire. Transformations are positive and life changing. It's like the caterpillar changing into the butterfly and freed from its prison on the ground. It soars out of its protective skin to greater heights. Happiness and contentment comes with change even if the change is unwanted initially. Everything is well in the end.

Abundance Exercise

Sit or stand in a stance of perfect contentment. You can do this anywhere. Sit or stand in front of a burning candlelight, or in a nature setting. Light some incense and play some soft music if you're at home. Take several deep-exhaling breaths. Recite affirmations surrounding any areas of blocks you'd like to release from your aura. You can say something like:

1.   *I wish to release any blockages within and around me.*

2.   *I wish to release any blockages preventing me from achieving success.*

3.   *I wish to release any blockages preventing me from obtaining that great love relationship.*

Stand or sit with your legs slightly apart. Spread your arms out slightly apart. Cup your hands together as if you have a bird sitting in it. Lift your hands into the air as they're cupped together and say:

"I accept abundance from the universe gracefully and without fear or guilt of receiving. I am deserving of the incoming gifts of abundance."

Chapter Eleven

Addictions, Attitudes, Leprechauns and Mystic Angels

Wise Ones have an inner tugging to accomplish something great at an early age. They're the ones that were thinking of leaving the nest by the time they were eight years old. They would be able to figure out how to survive on the streets if it came to that. They have natural street smarts having been around the block numerous times. This is not only in their current human life, but other lifetimes past. They've chosen to incarnate into an Earthly life more than those from any other Realm. This is why they sometimes give the impression of having gained knowledge of several lifetimes. These are the Children that have something profound about them. They appear otherworldly and *all knowing*. This attracts in taunts from lesser evolved Children and Adults who might tease the soul out of ignorance. Perceptive souls notice that the Wise One comes off well read at any age.

Wise Ones may have been around the block in the literal sense by having slept with a variety of people at some point in their life. Some have even fallen into the realms of sex addiction. Don't mistake sex addiction where one may cheat on their partner. The Wise One has too high of a standard to resort to infidelity regardless if the addiction gene is there. They are loyal and demand nothing less from others. If they don't get it, they might lash out. The Wise One may come off debonair, sweet and charming at times, but somewhere within them is a toughness demanding a somewhat high ethical code of etiquette. They're the guys that will correct someone's statement without apology.

An Incarnated Angel may indulge in food addictions to mask their sensitivity from the harsh energies of the world, but the Wise One indulges in addictions that include drugs, alcohol, love relationships and sex to numb their aura. Because of their street-smart toughness, they come with a back story of having done things that others might flinch at or be offended by.

One thing to note is that the Wise Ones are not typically lifelong addicts. They might be prone to addictions and may even have stories where they overindulged as an addict in some form, yet their calling is so strong that it overpowers and eventually triumphs over the addiction at some point in their life. This is by eliminating the addiction or keeping it so under wraps that no one notices when they indulge in the addictive substance once in a blue moon. This is not typically the case when it comes to the Incarnated Angels or Incarnated Elementals, who both may be prone to an addiction that carries through the duration of their Earth life. They have a rougher time trying to control the addiction.

This isn't to say that all those from a realm are addicts of course, but being a highly tuned in sensitive sponge prompts you to want to quiet the hyperactive feelings or thoughts. You might go through a period of indulging to cover it up. Star people are generally the most straight-laced and the least of the Realms to fall into a toxic addiction. They may be the ones that say, "Oh I tried some weed once and it didn't really do much for me. I never had the urge to try it again." Whereas the Wise One and Elementals have the opposite effect and should take caution they do not abuse negative substances. You're needed at this time to contribute positive changes and when you fall into a pattern of abusing addictive substances, you cause a delay in getting to work. Getting to work is also for your benefit as when you are focused, you are more apt to put in the work that attracts in the abundance of joy, peace and love you desire within.

Because the Wise Ones and Elementals reside so close to the Earth and in nature, some of them would be happy bathing in a tub full of marijuana plants. Not literally of course, I'm merely illustrating the differences in how some of the Realms are with certain things. The Wise One and Elementals are the ones attempting to get legislature to legalize the plant. They are likely the ones to say, "It comes from the ground and isn't tampered with by human souls, and therefore it is of God." They have a different kind of soulful spiritual connection with it. Think of the image of Wise One, poet and artist, Bob Marley.

I've had others ask how Heaven feels about Marijuana, since most people know how some human souls feel about it. Heaven is indifferent to human souls using weed. It is true it does come from the ground and is more natural than a burger at a fast food joint. The spirit world does not want to talk you in or out of doing something. They always insist that you remain as clear minded as possible to accomplish your goals and manifest happiness. It's understood that falling into any kind of addictive behavior is in order to feel closer to God, whether you're a believer or not. Addictive behaviors block positive manifestations to you and can also crumble your loving connections with family, friends and lovers. Heaven says that those who use weed will feel as if they are connected to God when they otherwise wouldn't be when sober. The reason this is the case is because your soul feels temporarily relaxed and released. The relaxing and releasing feelings are the state one would need to be in to pick up on accurate messages, feelings and thoughts with their Guides and Angels. The voices of the ego usually quiet down in that instant. Your vibration rises slightly and temporarily.

The issue is that the effects of weed eventually wear off leaving you feeling lethargic and unmotivated. Depression rises out of this feeling and you want to use again. It soon becomes an addiction. When you wake up the next morning after using, your vibration has dropped lower than it was before you used the substance. Not to mention you've forgot the messages that might have come in through Divine Guidance while in the drug high.

This is much like when you're in a dream state. When you go to sleep at night, your ego tends to move out of the way and your subconscious connects to the other side. This is how some have prophetic dreams that include messages from their Guides and Angels. When you wake up the next morning, your state of being and vibration has dropped to where it was before you went to sleep. This is the same concept as someone who smokes weed every night just for the fun of it and not for medical reasons instructed by their Doctor. Heaven says that the state you need to connect with them is built within your soul's DNA to do it naturally. Please note that if you use weed that we are in no way suggesting you stop or start, and nor are you being judged. We're merely discussing the positive and negative effects it has. You own your soul and your body and have free will choice. It is up to you to decide what you choose to do with the information or to disregard it.

One thing to note is that the blended Realms have a bit of some of the other Realms within them so they carry half of the traits, while not all of them. For example, someone incarnated from the Realm of the Leprechauns is half Wise One and half Elemental. They have a little bit of both of those two Realms.

Interesting to note when we stated that both the Wise Ones and Elementals have a penchant for addictions to drugs and alcohol. Notice that the Leprechaun has both elements of the Wise One and Elemental in them. Leprechauns are known to love their alcohol! The incarnated Leprechaun is sometimes what you would expect in appearance. They may have the red hair, be on the shorter end of height and love to drink! Not all Leprechauns have this look in the traditional sense. Some can be tall with dark or lighter hair such as actors, Colin Farrell, Robin Williams or Jeremy Renner. Leprechauns always seem to make it to a bar regularly or become a permanent fixture. Getting through a month without having one beer might be challenging for the Leprechaun.

Leprechauns have the fun and spark of the Elementals on one day, but then the next day they vacillate to the brooding seriousness of the Wise One. Their moods are always fluctuating back and forth from the fun to, "Stay away from me!" There is also the noticeable twinkle in their eye that comes from the Elemental realm. Leprechauns can be male or female. If they do not have red hair, they might have it in their genetics tree somewhere as far back as centuries.

Robin Williams had that warm mischievousness in his eyes that dance with humor. He vacillates from the practical joker to the deathly serious. This is evident in many of his film choices. He's played the fun, lighthearted Elemental type roles such as *Hook, Popeye, Aladdin, Jumanji* and *Mrs. Doubtfire* to the serious Wise One teaching roles in *Awakenings, Dead Poet's Society, What Dreams May Come* and *Good Will Hunting*. Like the Leprechaun, Robin has also battled with alcohol addiction most of his life. He's teetered on that fine line of presenting the light while battling the internal dark.

The Mystic Angels are half Wise One and half Incarnated Angel. They are the angels who morphed into the Wise One form while the Leprechauns are the Elementals who morphed into Wise One form. Mystic Angels have the sensitivity of the Incarnated Angel, but not as much as the Angel. They also have the toughness of the Wise One, but not as much. Some of them struggle with weight issues like the Incarnated Angel, but with the dark or intense eyes of the Wise One. Because the Mystic Angels have a little bit of both of those Realms in them, they also vacillate from co-dependency and neediness, to being independent without any attachments to anyone. It's a fun roller coaster ride for a Mystic Angel. They might be the cursing psychic with the tattoos and a cigarette dangling from her mouth. A

Mystic Angel would be someone like talents such as Johnny Depp, Demi Moore, Channing Tatum, Megan Fox, Margaret Cho, Christina Aguilera, Shia LaBeouf, Mila Kunis, Curtis Jackson (aka rapper 50 cent) or Joaquin Phoenix.   One thing those talents have in common is they have the Wise One's brusqueness to their aura's, but with the Incarnated Angels sensitivity.

The Mystic Angels and the Knights Paladin both have the half Wise One and half Incarnated Angel element in them. The difference is the Mystic Angels have a higher degree of Incarnated Angel in them while the Knights Paladin have a higher degree of the Wise One.

The Knights Paladin inherited the Wise One's strength and honor, while keeping the Incarnated Angel's compassion. The Mystic Angels inherited the Wise Ones mysticism and toughness qualities, while keeping the sensitivity of the Incarnated Angel.

The more challenging aspects they inherited were as follows: The Knights Paladin can be a little co-dependent on a partner almost smothering them, which is a trait inherited from the Incarnated Angel. The Knights Paladin goes into a possessive or jealous rage when slighted. This was inherited from the Wise One. The Mystic Angels tend to doubt, fear and second-guess themselves, which is an Incarnated Angel trait. They've inherited the non-censoring foul mouth and addictions of the Wise One.

The Upbringing of the Wise One

I've always been aware of the Realm world, although what my Spirit team had previously shown me through visual cues didn't have names attached to these images. On the other side they're not calling each other with the labels that we need here in order to identify the different groups. The Realm labels are good positive labels though.

It's not unusual for those in the Wise One realm to have had a difficult human upbringing. I personally grew up at the hands of an abusive parent. This is the one who blamed everything that went wrong on me. It was irrelevant if I had nothing to do with it or wasn't around when an incident happened. I was forced to endure it and take it. I learned to go along with it to make sure everyone was kept happy. Strangely enough I didn't feel any guilt or self-blame throughout that chapter of my childhood life. There was a period where I felt responsible for other people's happiness. This was just to keep them quiet and keep the peace. This doesn't necessarily have anything to do with the Wise One nature. The Wise One part of me made sure I didn't crumble or resort to self-blame. This had more to do with survival and what was hammered into me at the time. At this point, it was so long ago that it feels like it was another lifetime ago. Since Wise Ones might live several lifetimes in one it often feels like situations that took place were centuries ago.

Luckily and thank God, something miraculous happened as I aged and matured. The Wise Ones confidence grows to be off the charts. This is to the point where they no longer take responsibility for anyone's happiness, but their own. It reaches a point where they do not care, nor are they interested in the drama of others. They move into this space where it is everyone else who has the issues. They're sympathetic to others genuine pain, but they have a remote detachment to it. They ignore any and all drama and noise that comes from others.

The soul that was my Father in this particular lifetime was from no realm and he never fulfilled his purpose while here. Passing away from this lifetime in November 2010, he operated mostly from ego, although he loved the family unit and his children. He was a young baby soul who realized the truth as I discovered through my channel connections with him. He's had the opportunity to come to this realization and made amends. When he crossed over, he was brought through what is called the "Back Gate" of Heaven. This was a two year process in Earth years to get through.

My mom is still here on Earth at the time of this book. She is an Incarnated Angel and I've known this since I was a child. She is also a natural clairsentient, intuitive and Empath. Her sensitivity is high and off the charts. She's admitted from time to time that she never felt comfortable being here on Earth and that she was ignored by other Children growing up. When she was seventeen she got into an abusive co-dependent relationship with the man that would be my human father in this lifetime. These are all common gifts, issues and traits associated with an Incarnated Angel.

As a Wise One, I inherited my Mother's sympathetic *clair* traits along with heightened *clairaudience* and *claircognizance*. It was almost as if my *clairs* expanded from what she has. I had a detachment to an extent with both of my parents. As I grew into my 20's, our relationships improved and became more like a friendship and confidante situation. I was the go to person for any issues they had about anything or needing answers to something they didn't understand. I felt like I was the parent and they were the child by the time I was eighteen.

When I was seven years old, I had already started saying that I was ready to move out and be independent. I would've if it were legal! I became an adult before I was ten years old. My parents restricted me and blocked me from independent movement. In hindsight, they did not do it intentionally, but naively. I rose pretty quickly to independence that they didn't really have much of a choice, but in the end they were impressed instead of concerned. This includes my father who shifted from being an abusive person as he moved into his 40's.

My mother had commented once on what I was like when I was a young child of maybe five years old. She said whenever someone would grab my hand to cross the street for example, that I would yank it away. When someone would walk over to hug me, I'd turn around and walk away. From a very young age I was already asserting my independence that was part of my Wise One make-up to begin with.

By the time I was eight years old, I didn't feel the need to answer to any adult. Many Wise Ones evolve quickly within one lifetime. They might not be well liked as they're growing up because they toot their own horn. The lower selves in the human condition find that anyone who doesn't follow the norm, or the herd, is unusual. Wise Ones, or those from any realm for that matter, might have likely been teased at one time or another that they're so weird. By the time the Wise One has reached twenty years old, they are already displaying some of the markings of someone who is destined for greatness. They end up rising to the top and controlling or being in charge of those who might have poorly attempted to stop them.

The Opposing Opposites of the
Wise One and Incarnated Angel

Incarnated Angels have a huge dose of empathy and usually put their needs last. Wise Ones have that *me-first* attitude which is the ego to a degree, except Wise Ones have compassion and care about others to an extent. It may not come out in the outpouring sympathy some people crave. They keep a reserved wall up that's just large enough to prevent themselves from being buried in someone else's baggage and drama. The Incarnated Angel will be all in someone's business more than any other Realm.

Incarnated Angels are highly sensitive sponges. A Wise One is a sensitive sponge, but they mirror back what others are giving, which an Incarnated Angel doesn't do. An Incarnated Angel will absorb it and hold onto it. They tend to need a lot of space from their relationships and Wise Ones don't need that unless they're involved with a draining partner. If this is the case, the fights and unfriendliness may be epic!

Incarnated Angels feel responsible for other people's feelings and Wise Ones don't feel that kind of responsibility or care to that degree. An Incarnated Angel will allow relationships and friendships to get too heavy, too close and too fast. Wise Ones are difficult to get close to even when someone is close. They take forever to get remotely close to anybody and an Incarnated Angel jumps right in with full trust. The Wise One will be the one to wag a finger and say, "You can't trust anybody, but yourself." Wise Ones find themselves in a counseling role by default. Sometimes it gets to the point where others dump their emotions and problems on them. The Wise One loves to teach and instruct. However, if someone continues to use the Wise One as a filter to dump their problems onto, then they will unleash the Wise Ones hellish anger.

There was this beautiful lovely woman who I kept crossing paths with on the sidewalk in a little beach town in Southern California. She had additional weight on her, which can sometimes happen to an Incarnated Angel. At one point when I nearly ran into her again. Her smile and eyes lit up and she said, "Hiiii." Her voice was upbeat, warm and super genuine. She really wanted to get to know me. I was dead serious like the Wise Ones can appear and I put my hand out introducing myself. I immediately got a major hit and heard the words, "This is an Incarnated Angel!"

I said to her, "I know who you are. I scared you the other day when I came out of the dark around the corner and almost knocked you over. I apologize for that." We had a laugh.

I later thought, "Wow that was an Incarnated Angel! She found me." Those in the Realms are finding one another if even in passing to say hello. They are magnets bumping into one another in some manner for a purpose. We are all family after all even if we're spread out on the Earth plane.

The night I had almost run her over when I came around the corner on foot, I had a black sweatshirt hoodie on. The hood was over my head just like some dark Wise One with a cloak might have or wear. I was moving very quickly which is often how a Wise One might move about threading through a crowd. When I came around the bend, she jumped, grabbed her heart and then laughed. I pulled my hood down, half smiled and said, "Sorry." She continued on her way still laughing. I thought, "Hmm, she seems warmhearted."

Wise Ones usually wear dark clothing, or they like to cloak themselves. Some of this is because it's how they are in the Spirit World, but there are other factors that add to this. Their subconscious sees the cloaking as a way to ward off harsh energies. It also enables them to feel invisible while only appearing when they want. This is how they move about in the Spirit world. There is a darkness and heaviness about them. They witness the destruction of Earth in this life and previous lifetimes. They do not take this lightly and their dark style of dress at times is mirroring the darkness of humanity as well. The wardrobe colors lean towards earth colors, or the black, blue, green, grey, brown and violet shades. Some of them may wear heavy clothing even when their dress doesn't match the season. This isn't to say that Wise Ones never dress in flashier colors on occasion. On the contrary, sometimes they do enjoy shining if only once in awhile. This is when they appear breathtaking and stunning, but for the most part the colors they choose to wear are of the grounding Earth color variety.

Chapter Twelve

Retreats and Work Life for the Wise One

Wise Ones are comfortable with change just as long as the change is for the better. They will be hesitant to sway to change if they're unsure about something. They will weigh the pros and cons of a decision to the point of nitpicking. They love to take time out in nature, but there is an inner pulling that could make it difficult for some of them to relax. This takes some effort, even though they may preach it and endorse it. They insist that everyone take regular "time outs', and this goes for themselves as well! Wise Ones crave relaxation, but they do not seem to make enough time to do it often. They live by the clock and feel like they're racing against time. They've known from an early age that they're only here for a short amount of time and they don't want to waste it or take any minute for granted.

Even when a Wise One takes the time out to head into nature, they may not always be sitting! They're likely jumping, climbing, walking, jogging, rock climbing, biking, rowing or any other physical activity. Many of the Wise Ones on the other side are used to flying around and in motion, therefore it is not surprising to see the incarnated Wise Ones to be into physical activity. They're the guys that always appear to be thinking, in deep thought, or turned on.

The Knights Paladin, are the half part Wise Ones who are also big on exercise or physical activity. They'll be the stuntmen or those dare devils that have no problem jumping out of a plane. Wise Ones usually have a strong body, even if they might seem on the smaller end or appear frail while in a human body. When you look closer, you realize they are quite strong! This is regardless of their age in human years. Your age in human years becomes obsolete once you depart and head back home anyway. Ageism issues are a man made ego design.

If something needs to be done or completed, a Wise One has a difficult time stopping to relax. They have to keep going until it's done, and then they can relax. When a Wise One does take relaxation time, they don't have much guilt about it. They will temporarily shut off all outside responsibilities, lists and practicalities and enjoy the rare moments of relaxation. They might still be consciously aware of it in the back their mind. *"Okay, I have four hours to do this relaxing thing before I have to...."*

Wise Ones either have or prefer a dwelling that is outside of the big, bad city. Their dream residence is somewhere in a nature locale, just like the Incarnated Elementals. If Wise Ones had the choice and option they would like the best of both worlds. This would be a home that is nestled comfortably within a mountain range next to the beach. These settings remind them of their dwellings in the Spirit World as described in the beginning of the book. They need calm, peace and serenity. Some of them have those mechanical waterfalls or fountains in their backyards, rooms or offices. This reminds them of being back home with all of the waterfalls scattered about. Nature keeps your equilibrium in balance and your connections with the other side stronger. Wise Ones are more focused than usual in those settings. Many of the Wise Ones over history were the Native American Shamans and Sages. They were most comfortable living out in the open in the long stretches of nature land with little to no people. Even though the Wise One has no problem coming out of hiding every now and then to take the stage and conduct a seminar.

Wise Ones prefer warm, sunny, hot and happy weather. They don't mind the desert in the heat of Summer. They also love the Fall when the weather is still super warm and you have the desert breeze winds blowing through. Luxurious and awesome natural clear breathable weather outdoors is heaven to both Wise Ones and Incarnated Elementals.

Incidentally, the Aladdin Genies have 1/3 Wise One, 1/3 Elemental and 1/3 Angel. They draw some of the warmth from the Wise Ones in their craving for the desert and mountain-esque heat. They have the flashiness of the Elementals and sweetness of the Angel. They may wear a bright red shirt that someone can see for miles, whereas a Wise One would never believe they could pull that off. The Aladdin is the one who is constantly moving their place of residence. This is like the mythological images of the Aladdin on a magic carpet flying all over the place. A Wise One tends to stay put unless their purpose requires that they travel to various locations for work.

Wise Ones want to dive into their life purpose full time and immediately. They are more apt to knowing what their life purpose is before any other soul. They sense an inner tugging pushing them from an early age to get to work! If a Wise One is working a job where they feel stuffed in a cubicle or cold airy office five days a week and eight hours a day, their soul will feel dejected and they will crumble little by little. This is not healthy since your state of being will mirror an even bigger problem. This *breaking your back* kind of work for a paycheck will be too heavy on the Wise One's heart, breaking it metaphorically and literally. Wise Ones have been prone to heart attacks, often checking out of this Earthly life early due to this heaviness and stress. This is why Wise Ones should do their best in finding work that is meaningful to them and one that brings them uplifting pure joy. Also, be sure to incorporate relaxation activities into your constant on the go work ethic. Meaningful work is one that has a set up that is conducive to your equilibrium. If you do work in such a setting, make a pact to take long weekend trips to somewhere quiet for at least once a month if possible.

Throughout all of my work life, I have connected with all of my superiors and formed lifelong friendships with many of them. Wise Ones are leaders and can be authoritative in business. They prefer to work independently without the micro managing of a boss. In fact, if they don't feel a rapport with their boss, they will likely leave the job sooner than later.

One of my many gig's in the entertainment business was working with, Kate, a Hollywood Film Producer, who was Michelle Pfeiffer's producing partner for ten years in the 1990's. One of Kate's daughters was visiting the office with her one afternoon. The girl was eight years old at the time. I was passing through the hall where Kate was talking to her daughter. Kate saw me and she formed a huge smile, "Kevin. My daughter said something interesting today." She looks at her daughter, "Why don't you tell Kevin what you said to me this morning?" Her daughter blushed and hid behind her. I smiled and said, "She's shy." Kate said, "She goes, 'Mom are you the boss or is Kevin?'"

We both laughed not surprised. The lines are so blurred by how I take charge and control. Apparently, when I would engage with my boss in a business setting, I came off more authoritative than my superior! Others in passing who were not initially sure what our job titles were had the natural assumption that I was the top executive. The Wise One gives off this illusion because the work is done before you open your mouth. Most bosses who have an employee who is a Wise One will comment that they never have to micromanage that employee. The employee is so independent that there are no worries.

We were in Post Production on a popular film. I was continuing to handle the day-to-day logistics in terms of the movie making process. One day, the head of the Post Production team confessed something to me. He was working on the main titles of the film and going through all of the approvals for it. He said that as he was finalizing it that he didn't see my name. I said, "I'm in the end titles, not the main titles." After working with me for two months he admitted that he thought I was one of the Producers. The reason is I seemed to have the answers for everything regarding the picture even

121

over some of the other Producers! He then said, "They should be putting you in the main titles."

An Associate Producer on another film had also commented, "They should be giving you a higher title on this movie." I was perfectly pleased with being the Producer's Assistant. I knew it wasn't going to be lifelong work. It was a stepping-stone to writing books, which is my long-term purpose. This was another example of how to tell who is from a tribe of the Wise Ones. They are often in control, having the answers to things, and carrying themselves as if they're in charge, that most believe them to be the boss. That is until they discover the shocking truth that they are just the "star employee"!

The Wise One's purpose is neglected when they have other human obligations that need to be taken care of to survive first. This only leaves them a little bit of time to dabble into their purpose here and there. To the Wise One, this is frustrating and wasting a lot of their time here. They are aware that they don't have a lot of time in this lifetime and find it to be a waste diving into meaningless pursuits. They feel as if they are racing against time every single day that is spent partaking in time wasting activities, which includes working a mundane job they have no passion for. It is irritating to a Wise One that so much time is wasted on obligations that are practical in order to be able to do the life purpose work.

Wise Ones teach and instruct in the name of Light. Even if they are not a big believer in Heaven or the other side, there are still undertones within the work they're doing that point to metaphysics, philosophy and improving other human souls. Because most Wise Ones have a high degree of claircognizance, the non-believers of Heaven in the Wise One mix are unaware they are receiving divine information. Some of them love to spend time getting out there in the world and helping those who need it. Wise One, Mother Teresa, had an inner calling to travel and investigate areas where people were suffering. She wanted to contribute something positive to improving those situations. She would target the areas where humanity has lost its life force and instead choosing to act out in inhumane ways. Wise Ones were also people like genius, physicist Albert Einstein who received scientific messages and guidance from the other side through his *claircognizance* channel. There was also Walt Disney, who was a creative genius who received repeated psychic hits and visions of dreamy fairy tale like worlds that come from subconscious memories of the Wise One Kingdom in Heaven. Check out his history in bringing this to life through theme parks and films during the days when he was living an Earthly life. Let's not forget, Wise One Jesus Christ, a profound healer and teacher of God that continues to carry on indefinitely.

Chapter Thirteen

The Wise One
Counselor

Wise Ones are naturally claircognizant and therefore tend to be approached by friends, family members, acquaintances and strangers regularly seeking information or wisdom. Many human souls have been guided to me at the time they're about to experience relationship turmoil or heartbreak. The crumbling of their relationship shows cracks in its weak foundation by the time they reach out to me. They're seeking out anyone they can communicate to on how to save their current love relationship or find out what's wrong with it. They might want to know why their needs are not being met by the person they have an interest in romantically. This is about the time they stumble upon me and reach out hoping I can help them.

The Wise Ones are aware that they are the end of the road and the last resort for this soul. I am not intended to give this person a psychic read or coax them on in applause, yet it is what they secretly desire. The truth is that if this psychic reading were to take place, they would more than likely not receive the answer they hope for. This is why they have reached out to me in one final ditch effort to begin with. They have been guided to me by their own Spirit team. To this soul, I miraculously appear just as they needed it. Wise Ones are a symbol of strength and make excellent counselors. Souls who reach out to the Wise One tend to protest at some point that they have never felt so close to someone as they do with you. Their ego denies the real reason you have crossed paths. They reach out hoping I will say, "Yes! You two are meant to be TOGETHER! You have my full support! Give it time and be patient!" They are in a fragile state and their ego is not in a position to hear that what I truly "see" is that their relationship is on its final leg. It is reaching completion and they will need to adjust to this shift.

There are cases where I explain that the way their relationship is now will not sustain the distance unless they make necessary modifications to it. Unfortunately, what I notice is that the guidance is not followed because they tend to make the same mistake I warned them against doing. They come rolling right back around to me even more distraught. I repeat the same message I previously told them, hoping it will sink in. Eventually I begin to notice the trend of where their love connection is going as well as our false friendship connection.

The reason I appear just as they need it is because that is one of the roles that Earth Angels often play without asking for it. This is regardless if the Earth Angel is a Wise One, Incarnated Angel, Star Person, Incarnated Elemental or any other realm blend. All Earth Angels from the various Realms have specific purposes that they specialize in on the other side. They bring these gifts with them in the human body to perform important tasks for humanity. They are of service as all souls must be, including the new souls experiencing their first Earthly life.

Someone who feels hurt that their love partner is not measuring up to expectation is not going to feel the loving presence of their Spirit Guide and Angel. Those who incarnate from a realm give other souls a measure of hope. They give them comfort by acting in place of the all-knowing Light. Often Earth Angels will hear other souls cry out to them at some point, "If you weren't here, I would not know what I would do! I could not get through this without you!"

The human soul crosses path with me at the time they are experiencing a grieving ending of any kind, but typically around the issues of love relationships. This knowledge about love is embedded in my soul's DNA. Wise Ones are used to being the go to person for advice, guidance and wisdom. Sometimes the soul seeking assistance pushes their way into the life of the Wise One. They carefully make the Wise One their new private counselor, in order to discuss their current ongoing troubles with free of charge. Those from the realms are innately aware that these particular situations are a dangerous one-sided connection the majority of the time. The human soul using you as their own personal advice column believes you to be the best of friends! They do not yet know that this mirage of a friendship will one day end after they recover from the relationship turmoil they're in the middle of. This human soul loses control and dumps their current problems on you on a regular basis. Everyone experiences someone like this with others from time to time, or at some point in their lives. However, with those incarnated from the various realms, this is a regular occurrence throughout the duration of their Earthly life where they are the designated go to person for help. The human soul who has appeared as your new case comes to you in a broken state. This would be considered highly unusual for outsiders to assume you're becoming best friends, because in truth you are a stranger or acquaintance to this person.

This is why all Earth Angels must shield and guard their souls and the space around them. You cannot afford to allow regular amounts of toxin into your vicinity. Toxins do come in the form of complaints and negative words. This person is using you to complain about their problems on a regular basis. They are innocently transmitting these toxins into your space. You must keep some measure of distance and beware of getting too close or you will be pulled under as many from the realms can attest. It is okay to assist the person to a degree, but be mindful that you do not become caught up and consumed in the other person's drama permanently. This is especially the case if the drama that the soul is experiencing is prolonged for a long period of time. Not only do they continue to suffer, but you end up suffering by absorbing these toxins. Some souls choose to live in misery in an unhappy relationship connection and they will continue to complain about it. No matter what advice or guidance you give them, they are not interested in leaving the toxic love relationship. The partner they are complaining about usually will abruptly leave them.

You are a temporary friend to this person, even if they feel that you have a much deeper friendship. Remember that real friendships are when you both have similar interests in activities and values. You have similar communication styles and you do things together as friends. They are also a listening ear to you in equal amounts. It is not you being a listening ear every time this soul reaches out to you to dump their problems onto. A genuine reciprocated friendship is not going to form due to someone reaching out to you for shotgun advice on a whim. They latch onto you believing you have a deep friendship, when this is not the case.

The majority of time this soul reaches out to you is for your assistance or advice on a toxic relationship they're involved with. This is sucking high vibrational energy out of your spirit while lowering your vibration every time they contact you. Being a loving light soul, you naturally want to help, but you will experience the downside to this. You will discover that months have passed, and perhaps even years, and this person is still complaining to you about the same ongoing problem. You discover that you're trapped and need to figure out how to wiggle out of this person's claws. This soul is resisting the truth that their love relationship is on a decline and will soon end. They will feel deeply broken hearted, but Wise Ones know that the soul must move into that doorway of change where brighter prospects will surface. This soul was not truly happy in their current relationship to begin with. Otherwise they would not have reached out to you repeatedly in the first place. They will come to the realization that their connection is indeed over, or has been over for longer than they'd care to admit to.

If someone complains about their love relationship more than they say good things about it, then this is a sign that the relationship is over. It does not meet their needs and desires in a relationship. Their love partner is not going to suddenly display a miraculous turn around. They might show signs of improvement, but it is not long before they're reverting right back to their bad habits.

Relationships are about compromise, work and communication. If you do not put in the work and neither party puts in an effort, then the relationship will soon crumble. Compromising is accepting that your love partner is a certain way and is not going to change. It is both partners meeting half way by adjusting their nature to one another. If you're unable to fold on that, then the relationship will eventually end and not peacefully.

One of my roles has pushed me to be present during this relationship ending until they realize that the love relationship they are in is over. This is when I notice the connection they have with me begins to dissolve as well. There are cases where you and this other person who has reached out to you are experiencing a love relationship ending at the same time. You are brought to one another to be a supportive soul mate to each other in the form of a friendship. Once you have both made your peace with the love relationship ending, then the friend soul mate connection typically begins to dissolve or lessen as well. There are rare exceptions, but this is about recognizing where the exception is not the case. It is important as a Wise One to keep some measure of distance when assisting others. Wise Ones are incredibly difficult to fool and can see through someone trying to take advantage of them. Exercise emotional detachment from other people's drama. Avoid becoming stuck in the role of permanent counselor to someone, unless you are a paid counselor, psychic reader, or healer and it is your career practice. Those who are paid professionals have strict etiquette rules where the client needs to make a paid appointment if they are experiencing life troubles.

Chapter
Fourteen

The Wise One Talent
in Entertainment

In this Chapter, we'll look at several well-known actors in Cinema history who are indeed from the Realm of the Wise Ones. This is to give you additional examples on how to tell who falls into this realm. It's also easy to look them up if you've never heard of them and examine their history and personal lives. Many Wise Ones are not just highly psychic sages and ministers. Wise Ones show up on the big screen in movies. They've come here for the purpose of bringing joy and release by playing characters in a compelling movie.

Wise Ones are attracted to darker content with an edge. They love strong, tough protagonists in entertainment, even if the main character is a killer! Wise Ones enjoy radical stories, messages and movies that showcase someone fighting against injustice. They enjoy movies that deal with serious relationship issues, dark content and strong characters. The strength, dark and fighting nature descriptions are words to describe the types of media entertainment they feel drawn to.

Wise Ones have a special love for all things dark when it comes to their entertainment choices. They may love movies like, *Bram Stoker's Dracula* to *Natural Born Killers*. Their tastes are rough and sometimes leading to the macabre. To them it's just everyday life while to others it may be too harsh. They're used to the darkness of reality. Wise Ones have been to battle in previous lifetimes and on the other side, therefore they don't flinch from the dark side of life. Even their humor is of the darker variety. They may be the one that laughs at something that no one else is laughing at because it feels politically incorrect. Wise Ones are on the serious side, but there are Wise Ones who have great humor within them. It's the Incarnated Elementals who are some of our most notable stand up comics, but the Wise Ones have the dark humor.

It's not usual for some of the Wise Ones to showcase this large humor on occasion beneath the layers of their disciplined seriousness. Director and Writer, Woody Allen is an example of a Wise One that focuses on long monologues that are mixed with seriousness at times and humor at other times. Wise Ones have a beautiful capacity to bring out both. They are born with an understanding of the human condition and have an innate attraction to solid love relationships and family units. They understand the human destruction to the stability of love in the current climate and know this is done by ones ego. They are able to bring this understanding of love and relationship dynamic out impeccably through their life purpose. If they're in the entertainment field, then they bring this out through movies, music or books.

Many of Cinema's most popular actors have incarnated from a Wise One Realm. They are here for the purpose of bringing love, joy and entertainment to other human souls. These performers have no problem diving into roles that are dark, tough and even antagonistic. Wise Ones slide comfortably into the shoes of a dark role more than once.

Actress and Activist, Angelina Jolie is the modern day Mother Teresa. She is another example of the image of a Wise One. This is evident in the history of her earlier years when she was experimenting with drugs, alcohol and sex. As she evolved and matured, it wasn't long before she went through a major transformation that was documented by the public. She is an A-list actress and was finding that the fame and attention seeking part of show business was rubbing her the wrong way. She used her celebrity status to bring light to the more serious issues happening in the world. This included rising to the prominent role of Goodwill Ambassador for the United Nations High Commissioner for Refugees.

As a Wise One, Angelina does not shy away from the harsh cruelty of war, darkness and inhumane acts in other countries. Others do not want to draw attention to the serious issues, but the Wise One blows it up right out in the open regardless. Angelina has written about her experiences in some of these countries in her book, "Notes from my Travels". Through the written word is a great way for the Wise One to teach and share your knowledge.

Angelina's film choices have reflected the personality of this realm too. A great deal of her films contains both the *dark* and the *action* in them. These films include, *Mr. & Mrs. Smith, The Bone Collector,*

Tomb Raider, Taking Lives, Salt, The Tourist, Maleficent, and *Wanted.* Add in the Femme Fatale qualities she exudes only further cements the allure and seductive qualities some Wise Ones have. Couple this with her fight on social issues in third world countries, and you can see how she managed to satisfy all parts of her Wise One nature through the choices in her life. The Wise One is loyal in love and family and she balances that out with all of the good a Wise One can do. She's also brought humanitarian movies to light such as, *A Mighty Heart, Changeling* and *Beyond Borders.* These films feature strong lead characters fighting for an important cause.

Her Wise One skills came into play again when she wrote and directed, *In the Land of Blood and Honey,* a dark love story about a soldier and a prisoner in the Bosnian war.

Her most notable role that connects closest to the Wise One is *Maleficent.* The Maleficent character has the Wise One love of magic, strength and darkness. This is intertwined with the fairy tale like world of the Elementals in the Wise One Realm. Although in the movie, she is a powerful Faerie, it's important to note that her characteristics are aligned with the Wise One rather than the Elementals.

When Maleficent is rejected and betrayed by her lover Stefan, she moves into the Wise One rage, which she hangs on for eons. Stefan betrays her in order to become a King through ego greed and power which the Wise One dislikes. Maleficent's rage is so dark and intense, that after having a quick cry, she flies off the handle and moves into anger, just like the Wise One. Stefan and his new Queen have a child and name her Aurora. Maleficent has been spying on Stefan for years still holding onto revenge. She casts a spell on Aurora when she's born. She throws out a magic spell so powerful that curses the child to fall to her death on her sixteenth birthday.

Maleficent develops a loving relationship with the child as she's growing up. This brings her to have a change of heart about the spell she cast. The problem is that she made the spell unbreakable even by her. This is what Wise Ones must be careful of. When they get angry, even if they're not practicing spell casters, they still have these manifestation capabilities. Some of this forms in their mind and is so powerful that they can cause harm just by thinking it.

Speaking of Angelina Jolie, Brad Pitt is also one who falls into the Realm of the Wise One. He has the deep, intense eyes of those in this Realm. This is an example of two Wise Ones teaming up in a love partnership. They both travel the world fighting important humanitarian causes together while bringing entertainment to the masses through Movies.

Entertainment was designed and created by many from the Realms, because the Angels know that entertainment has the capacity to heal other human souls. Movies can make you laugh, cry, experience and even have therapeutic healing qualities depending on the kind of movie you're watching. Many therapists have recommended that a client watch a particular movie to bring light to serious issues they may have trouble overcoming.

When Wise One actor, Russell Crowe isn't shooting movies, he's a great Philanthropist who donates his money to improve conditions in schools. His movies are a great place to see where his Wise One nature comes in. Russell has the intense, probing eyes with the lines of wisdom around them. He's played characters that touch on his Wise One nature. He's made movies where he's played an officer of the law with a dark side in *L.A. Confidential,* a warrior hero in *Gladiator,* fighting to take down a major corporation in *The Insider,* playing a Wise One genius in *A Beautiful Mind,* a physical fighting boxer in *Cinderella Man,* and a hunter with a bow and arrow in *Robin Hood.* He's played leaders in films where he was a Captain in *Master and Commander,* and a Wise One detective in *American Gangster, Les Miserables* and *Tenderness.* Russell has shown his Wise One romantic side in the simplified idealistic story amidst the backdrop picturesque beauty of Provence in *A Good Year.* All of this speaks to the soul part of his personal make-up.

Russell has an affinity and connection towards horses. These wild stallions subconsciously remind his soul of his days with the Unicorns on the other side. The public is not in the dark to know that Russell has a reputation of having a temper. The Wise Ones, as we've discussed, are prone to outbursts and becoming overbearing when angry. This is a fight they may not be proud of, but sometimes unable to control. Another Wise One actor has faced the same kind of temper behaving scrutiny. Christian Bale, like other Wise Ones, became overly heated, passionate and irate when believing with maximum intensity that someone had broken his focus on a movie set.

Christian Bale has the deep, dark intensely serious eyes that most Wise Ones have. Many of his film choices point to the Wise One energy. Bale had no problem slipping into the shoes of a narcissistic serial killer in the dark, bloody, *American Psycho.* Nor was he shying away from playing this intelligent, refined, yet dangerous and evil character. Christian chose to disappear and vanish into invisibility when he fought for justice as Batman in the *Dark Knight Trilogy*. He played a leader in a spiritual science fiction piece where his characters conscious is raised in *Equilibrium*. He's awakened his warrior qualities in *Terminator Salvation* and *The Fighter*.

Note that both Russell Crowe and Christian Bale had eventually portrayed characters taken from the Bible, Russell Crowe in *Noah* and Christian Bale as Moses in *Exodus: Gods and Kings*.

Like the Wise One, Noah, had prophetic clairvoyant visions and saw the worst in humanity believing they had no hope. This is a common complaint of Wise Ones, hence being called misanthropic by those lesser evolved.

It's important to look at what's beyond the film choices by an actor, and to examine the entire package. What are they like personally, their physical characteristics and what are their pursuits like.

Michelle Pfeiffer, just like the Wise One, has been notably uncomfortable with any public attention. This includes the attention to her physical beauty. Having worked with Michelle for her production company and on several of her films, I've had the privilege to watch her in action. She is known for playing strong characters and she's not afraid of dark material.

She's enjoyed playing roles where she can cloak herself into invisibility in roles like *Frankie & Johnny, Married to the Mob* and *New Year's Eve*. Yet, also like the Wise One, she enjoys the dark content in roles such as, *What Lies Beneath, Dark Shadows, Batman Returns, Wolf* and *White Oleander*. She's also managed to satisfy the Wise One's magic interests in witchcraft films like *Witches of Eastwick* and *Stardust.* She's also been drawn to being in movies with a social message such as *Hairspray, I Am Sam,* and *Dangerous Minds.*

In person, Michelle is a lot tougher than some might imagine. When she moves, it's much like a military sergeant with purpose swinging her arms from side to side with great intention. She moves in a way that prompts others to jump out of the way. She has the Wise One's no-nonsense attitude in business and she insists on only playing strong characters. Michelle has also got the Wise One's personality traits such as being dark, withdrawn and guarded. She's admitted to wanting to do an action film, which is also a Wise One trait especially if they're an actor. Action and conquering something takes them back home! She moved out of the superficiality and crowdedness of Los Angeles and headed up to Northern California in nature and quiet, but close enough to the bigger city if need be. Wise Ones crave a quiet, nature backdrop for their dwelling if they had the choice.

One thing to note about the four actors mentioned in this chapter is that they are all pretty hush-hush about their private lives as much as they can be. The Wise One prefers to do their work and do not necessarily crave media attention unless there is the added benefit of bringing their work to light.

There is one exception and that is the entertainer, Madonna, who falls into the Wise One Realm. You must examine all aspects of a soul beyond what Realm they come from. She was born under the astrological Sun sign of Leo. Leo's crave adoration on some level. Even though this is ego, it is astrologically enforced within their DNA. The challenge for them is to temper it as much as possible and keep it under control.

A Wise One doesn't fall into every single trait discussed in this book, but you're looking at the majority of the traits. Madonna has a hard work ethic and fighter nature that has spanned decades. She falls into the category of someone who would say, "Wow. She's done so much!" Wise Ones keep working until they drop. She has been known to be in complete control of her surroundings, career and life purpose. Her humanitarian interests grew over time to the point where she has continued to open up schools for the underprivileged. Higher learning, educating yourself and raising your consciousness is a big deal to her. She was considered an overachiever in High School. All of this points to the nature of a Wise One.

Her Spirit team asked her to incarnate into another human life. This would be to make a worldwide impact through music and entertainment. She shifted the perception of the business as a woman in control of her career when that was not the popular thing. She would attract an audience who wouldn't normally be spiritually awakened, but who just want to have fun. There is nothing wrong with wanting to have fun, but this Wise One injects the fun with the more serious issues.

Many pop stars come from the world of the Incarnated Elementals. These are the artists such as, Britney Spears, Justin Timberlake, Rihanna and Miley Cyrus. Miley Cyrus looks just like a little Pixie from the Elemental realm doesn't she? Lady Gaga falls into a blend of the category of Incarnated Elemental with a little bit of Star Person. The Star person influence is in the faraway look in her eyes. Her work has some of that far out Star and Atlantean influence too. Remember the image of her arriving at an awards show in an egg shaped vessel? Katy Perry is a blend of the Wise One and

Incarnated Angel falling into the category of Mystic Angel. She has the spiritual interests and dark, deep eyes of the Wise One with the sensitivity and relationship heartbreak of the Incarnated Angel. Let's also not forget Incarnated Elemental, Michael Jackson, whose biggest fight was towards saving the planet and the environment. This is a big deal to the Incarnated Elementals.

You may ask how is it those artists come from the Realm of the Incarnated Elementals or blended realms, but Madonna comes from the Realm of the Wise One? Remember that the Elementals and Wise Ones both mix and mingle with one another and have some similarities. The Incarnated Elementals love to dance, sing and party. Madonna has all of those qualities, but she is considered more authoritative, disciplined and having the stance of a General, especially on stage. This is the mark of a Wise One. Incidentally, Madonna was a male General in another life. She is also big on physical fitness. The humanitarian causes and charitable contributions she fights for and contributes to that most of the public is likely unaware of, push near the sixty mark and beyond. This is up there with Bono of U2 mentioned earlier in the book. This is in comparison to the other pop stars named that reportedly contribute to fewer charitable fights. There is no contest with what someone fights for, but the Wise One tends to take on quite a bit due to the engrained work ethic within them. There are other factors that point to her Wise One nature as well beyond what charities and fights one partakes in.

Her fight in the beginning of her career included pushing the images of sexuality, gender attraction and gender equality. This was during a time when others wouldn't have dared to do it. Now we see it regularly in all media, but at that time it was considered taboo. Now it's just out of control, but everything is due to the human ego abuse of media and technology. The Wise One does not shy away from shedding light onto controversial topics that would typically anger the world.

She has also been known to infuse spiritual and religious concepts somehow into her music, videos and concerts. The public is aware of her interest in the Kabbalah religion. She's pushed images of crosses and the use of guns and war on stage. And let's not forget her dominating temper when things are not perfect. These are all marks of a Wise One whose fight moves into the larger areas beyond just the music, and dance and into spirituality. Her romantic suitors have reportedly been younger than her or significantly younger, except for perhaps Warren Beatty. Even then, her soul was drawn to someone older and wiser for education purposes, in order to gain additional knowledge, since Wise Ones vacillate from the role of lifelong teacher and student. If you examine the Wise Ones, you'll notice the age gap in some of their relationships. This is not always the case, but there is a pattern where the Wise One tends to be the teacher in a teacher-student relationship dynamic. There isn't always an age gap and sometimes they are indeed the younger one, but still in the dominating teacher role.

With the case of Brad Pitt and Angelina Jolie, where both fall into the Realm of the Wise One, they have a twelve year age gap in human years between them. Like the Wise One, Madonna's underlying messages have always been Universal love and that all paths lead to love and God. When you ignore the public flogging and criticisms against her, which come from ego, then you are able to see that her fight has been to hammer home the joy and love essence throughout her music and career.

Other Wise Ones fall into some of our great classic rockers like Stevie Nicks, Steve Miller, James Taylor, Lindsay Buckingham, Alanis Morissette and Sheryl Crow. You'll note some of our classic rockers back in the 1960's and 1970's fell into drug and alcohol addiction, which is a dangerous habit for a Wise One.

Chapter Fifteen

No Tears for a Wise One

Wise Ones have lived so many lifetimes on Earth and on the other side that they are accustomed to the process of death. They are aware that when the human soul dies that this does not mean the end. They're usually not crying when there is a human death. If they do shed tears, it may last a short period, rather than for months at a time. Part of this has to do with this inner strength that has been part of their make-up before their human birth. They might be versed in spiritual practices such as Mediumship, where one is accustomed to communicating with those on the other side. It may be embedded in their subconscious from their memories of many lives before, or their life in the spirit realm. They are usually designated to the driver seat because of this seeming strength. This stems all the way back to childhood, rather than something that was gained due to other losses in their human life. This is a trait that is innate within their soul's make up on the other side.

What is interesting to note is the Wise One will cry over the loss of a broken relationship more than they will over a human death. Hence the image of Angelina Jolie in Maleficent wailing in tears when she discovers her lover betrayed her. Note she quickly rises to anger with the occasional blip of sadness creeping in. It takes so much for a soul to melt the walls of a hardened Wise One that when they allow trust and love in and they're betrayed, the feeling is too intense to comprehend. The betrayal alone is against the Wise One protocol. They're used to setting the incorrect behavior right in some way. They may wait years to correct it, but they will at some point. Their opponent may not know what hit them.

The Wise One always seems to be the listening ear whenever someone is upset, but they too have moments where they work themselves into the ground. Although rare, Wise Ones falter at times and break down. They suddenly crave a listening ear, affection or even a foot rub. Unfortunately, they come to the assumption that no one is capable of returning the favor at the capacity that they usually put in. Wise Ones are the guys who are not crying when there's a death. They're usually the rock and the ones that people are commenting in terms of their strength. "You are so strong!" It might seem odd that the Wise One will tear up at a movie or by hearing moving words said by someone, but a death not so much. It's not that the Wise One doesn't care or doesn't feel anything when there's a death. On the contrary, they have deep compassion and sympathy.

Hours after my father passed away in 2010, everyone banned together, 20-30 people, family, friends and business associates taking the day off to join in the grieving. Everyone is crying, upset or hysterical. I noticed a band of Paramedics and Police Officers all approaching me at once. One of them said, "Can we speak with you? You seem to be the only one here holding it together." I said, "Because a human death is not the end. They're just having a tough time wrapping their minds around that."

I was affected by my father's death inside and went through another transformation, but I did not break down. Those who do not know me would imagine I'm just holding it in or pushing it down, but if that were only the case. Goodbyes are difficult for human souls. It's understandable and I have compassion surrounding those who are grieving. It also makes it easier for others who are grieving to be able to come to me to talk it over.

I called a woman after her son committed suicide. She said, "I was going to call you. I thought, 'I've got to call Kevin. He is so stronggg'." The Wise One does not have much guilt when they notice that they're the only ones not producing tears. They know they can easily be there for others who are grieving. They have feeling and think about it, but it doesn't affect them the way it does others. When you have a connection with the process of life and where we go after this, it puts it all into perspective for them.

Chapter
Sixteen

Heaven is Real

If there are those who are jealous or threatened by you, then you must be doing something right. There isn't one person on the planet that is universally loved. Even deity's or the most popular artists in entertainment, or religious icons and healers have their detractors. You have to pay them no mind, stay focused and keep moving forward with what you need to do. There will be those who will pop up to attempt to antagonize you or your work from time to time. This is a given, but do your best to ignore it and remain detached from them. You don't need that energy or karma hanging around you.

I have the Warrior of Light aura around me, and the Wise One on top of that, and I'm also born during what some call the Indigo generation or Indigo energy. I'm a triple whammy magnet for detractors. I get my fair share of disparagers, but I do my best to pay no mind. I have a job to do while here and I work for the other side before anything or anyone else. When I'm done, I'll be out of here and that will be that.

I was reaching for something around one of my plants at home. Violet light surrounded the edges of every leaf. The plant was alive and blooming. It was looking more lush than usual. I knew that my third eye was showing me something. Some of the plant leaves were ruffling as if something was moving in it. Leaning in closer into the plant I saw a little fairy walking around the larger tree stem. She was translucent with sparkly gold and violet lights twinkling. I stood staring at her hypnotized with a weird look on my face. There was nothing gross about this fairy, but I was entranced. She was about 2 ½ inches high and not wearing much clothing. I had never seen a fairy through clairvoyance, although I do see the occasional angel lights in garden and park like settings. I knew that some of the angels have roles where they chose to be a nature angel overseeing Earth's wonders. Amidst them are the faeries as well. I remained skeptical as is typical of a Wise One questioning everything until they've experienced it.

I realized this particular Faerie swooped in to care for my plant during a time when I was working on this book. This is the first time that I've mentioned or even talked about Faeries. When you reach a place where you believe in their existence they will make themselves known. Faeries, being part of the Incarnated Elementals, have the largest ego as I've discussed. This means if you do not give them any attention, then they will not appear for you, or assist you in manifesting your physical material needs. They reveal themselves when you have shown yourself to be a caring individual activist when it comes to Nature. This means litterbugs can forget about running into a Faerie and receiving their practical assistance and insight. An angel does not hold such rigid rules, but the Faeries are not egoless like them. They have physical bodies the way some spirits do on the other side.

I remember seeing other people post images of Jesus Christ on a Unicorn in the past. This didn't offend me, but I thought it was a little silly and whimsical. That was until I was taken into the Realm of the Wise One world, where I have a best buddy as a Unicorn who I ride with, play with and communicate to. Before that moment, I had never believed in Unicorns or had an opinion on them. If Jesus is a Wise One as I've been told, then it's not out of the question that he has Unicorns and Horses around him as some believe. It's like the gaps and missing pieces are being filled. Now everything has changed. I've been shown more of the wonders of the Spirit world that has shifted my perception even more. There is no turning back now.

Is Heaven for real? The answer is yes. I know this because I've seen it on more occasions than I can count. I've experienced it and been taken through it. I blink my eyes and the various images and messages of the spirit world flash in front of me without warning and then evaporate. This has been going on for as long as I can remember. From the moment I was born, I had one foot in the physical world and the other foot in the world where I came from.

It's nothing like the statues of religious icons and imagery that human souls have developed over the centuries. Those images are cute and beautiful. It gives human souls hope and faith that there is something more than the struggling lives you might be currently living. It's nothing like that in the spirit world.

I've relayed descriptions of the other side sprinkled through several of my books. From my near death experience that cracked my portal open and shifted me down a holier path in *Reaching for the Warrior Within*, to the process your soul endures as it crosses over in *Warrior of Light*, to the differences between the souls in Heaven with those on Earth in *Empowering Spirit Wisdom*, and to the magical paradise of life in Heaven in this book, *Realm of the Wise One*.

There is something else beyond this dimension and I've been experiencing it throughout this current life. The glimpses they continue to give me while I'm here remind me of what's important and to ignore the cattle and noise of the human ego in the souls demanding attention. In comparison, the other world makes life on Earth trivial and more accurately aligned with Hell. Yet, there are glimpses of Heaven in its rarity attempting to shine its way through the thick thud of the aura of the state of the human body. If only human souls could keep their vibration high full time. What a peaceful, blissful and loving world this planet would be!

Chapter Seventeen

A Look at Some of My Guides and Angels

There are seven main Spirit Guides and Angels that are part of my Spirit team. This includes my one main spirit guide and one guardian angel. They have both been with me since birth as everyone has this same deal. The other guides and angels around me came in one by one as I was growing up. They've remained permanently by my side in my current lifetime. There is also Saint Nathaniel who has been with me since around 2009. I was about to embark on a major transition once the healing from a relationship was complete from that particular connection. Saint Nathaniel is the tough love messages I feature in some of my works on humanity as a whole. He is the warrior of light, Wise One and task master who instructs most of the harsh stuff on humanity I sometimes bring up.

There is no set pattern that is consistent in how Guides and Angels communicate, because other factors play a part in that. It's a frequency that is shifting up and down all throughout the day and everyday depending on what's going on in your world. What your guides say is on a need to know basis. I've had letters sent to me by others who say their Guides are expressing frustration with them because they're not listening. This is not a Guide, but the ego taking over. An angel or heavenly guide is not going to tell someone that they're not listening and that they're tired of telling someone what to do. If you believe that they're telling you this, then you would hear the rest of the information and not just the frustration language. Scolding is a lower energy or the ego taking over. Angels use high vibrational words and energy when they communicate. They heal, comfort, inspire and guide delicately and positively. They have an endless reserve of patience so it's not likely an angel who is getting frustrated, but the ego. It is also possible it can be a departed loved one, since they have a good measure of their human ego intact as they work to strip it away on the other side. If that's the case, then you'll want to request a higher vibrational guide and ask that the departed loved one be removed from the duties of assisting and guiding you.

There are other guides and angels that come in and out of my vicinity for different reasons, but the main seven, plus Saint Nathaniel are the permanent team that never leave or are close by. There are occasions where I'm communicating specifically with one who I've addressed directly. Depending on what's going on or what the situation calls for, the right guide or angel steps forward. They take turns orchestrating certain events that are in my favor. One guide may be working on bringing the next love mate to me, while another is working on the career or work stuff. Their goal is to ensure that I stay on path teaching, writing, inspiring and entertaining. I have long lists of things that need to be said and done. One guide is not enough for all of it.

There are times where they do speak in concert, except for Saint Nathaniel who works separately with me.

The names of my Spirit Guides and Angels around me are Luke, Enoch, Veronica, Matthew, Jeremiah, Samuel and Jacob. Saint Nathaniel sometimes known as Bartholomew leads the pack.

Luke is my main Spirit Guide and has been since my human birth in this lifetime. His main role with me was and has been my entire work and career life to date. Every job and work position I ever received since I was seventeen were all part of the plan to gain additional tools and knowledge that would lead to the role I am in now. Luke has been instrumental in this process and continues to be so. He works closely with Archangel Gabriel and Archangel Uriel who comes in when it comes to my writing and promoting my work.

Veronica is my main Guardian Angel and has been since birth. She has been the front and center angel that has kept me on a healthy path. I knew from the early age of eight the importance of exercise and health. This was instilled in me primarily from Veronica. There were times where I indulged in addictions that would lead to one poor situation after another. Both Luke and Veronica would scream through the thud to get me back on path as soon as possible. Luckily, I listened to my Guides and Angels, otherwise I may have checked out early.

As I grew to know my guides and angels, I discovered some interesting historical facts about them that they did not reveal immediately. The reason they often withhold information from you is for a variety of reasons. One of them is that sometimes it's a 'need to know' basis. Other times it can be that you may not be in a position to accept the answer.

Saint Nathaniel

Saint Nathaniel is one of the many Ascended Masters on the other side. Ascended Masters are also Saints who often act as spiritual teachers and guides to advancing or evolving student souls on Earth for specific purposes. This is when you are ready to take on a more serious role in this lifetime that entails helping others through communication, leading, teaching and inspiring. It is not uncommon for Wise Ones to have guides who are ascended masters. Nathaniel started popping in for me in a regular appearance in 2009-a catastrophic year for me personally. It was crucial in that it was the ending of another chapter part of my life. It was the final chapter of all my years up to that point. Nathaniel knew where I would be embarking to next, which was an entirely different book, rather than the next chapter. The life lessons, class and karmic debt were wrapping themselves up. My soul vibration was rising to a higher degree. I was climbing out of the confinement of my material body.

Nathaniel instructed that I move into the role of the empowering teacher that all of my guides had been showing me for the ten years prior, but my ego denied this. My work life would be shifting and I would go through a powerful spiritual transformation. This is described in my book, *Reaching for the Warrior Within.* My Spirit Guide Luke had informed me that November 2010 I experienced what someone might consider to be a near death experience while enduring a physical work out injury. This lasted for a millisecond in Earth time. Something shifted and turned in me where I would never be the same again after that month. This was simultaneous with the death of my father within that same month. This marked where my soul was freed and my former karmic debt officially paid off. I merged effortlessly and immediately into the role of a *Warrior of Light* full time. The change happened so gradually and fluidly by sheer magic. It was as if some strong force did something to my soul that profoundly shifted something within me at that point. I was awakened! My state of mind has been awesome ever since.

Saint Nathaniel appeared in 2009 just as the transition was about to happen in order to start aiming me in that direction. He knew what was coming. When I was on the other side, he and I, along with my other guides all discussed the agreement that included when they would reveal themselves to me during my Earthly run.

In the summer of 2011, I asked who was guiding me with all of this new stuff that I seemed to know involuntarily. He said his name was, Nathaniel. He didn't seem like the usual suspects around me, but instead came off quite stern and authoritative. His language had a biblical tone and was decoded into English in order for me to understand. It's like talking to someone with an accent. I asked why he sounds as if he is ancient. He informed me that he is not one of my guardian angels, but a hierarchy Saint and Ascended Master. He has been a crucial force in any and all words I utter that are aligned with humanity. Humanity is in desperate need of a *real awakening*. That is obviously coming from Nathaniel since before that point I could care less.

There was another spirit with the same energy as Nathaniel who started communicating with me around the same time. He said his name was, Bartholomew. Months later, I realized that Nathaniel was and is

Bartholomew. I didn't understand the point of the interchangeable name.

Nathaniel/Bartholomew ushered in the important messages in my previous spiritual books, *Warrior of Light: Messages from my Guides and Angels* and *Empowering Spirit Wisdom*. When those works were complete, he informed me in greater detail who he was in a human life. This was in order to not distract me from the work of those particular books.

Saint Nathaniel is from the tribe of the Wise Ones. He is known to some on Earth as one of the three Wise men who brought gifts for the celebration of the birth of Jesus Christ. To some he is known as one of the Twelve Apostles. It was suddenly all being pieced together for me. Some on Earth also knew Saint Nathaniel as Bartholomew in those ancient days. Saint Nathaniel is from the Realm of the Wise One and was a Wise Man on Earth. He's worked with Christ and was a well known astrologer in those days. All of these mark the traits of someone who is a Wise One. His authoritative teaching tone when he speaks, display a highly evolved Ascended Master.

When further discovering this information, my Guides and Angels pointed out who they were. They are prophets, angels and teachers from what some consider the biblical years. They have been referenced often in various philosophical texts.

Many prophets come from the Realm of the Wise One, so I did not find this surprising that they were my guides. Wise Ones in human form travelling with the big guns is not uncommon. Incidentally, Saint Nathaniel was known to have carried the Book of Matthew when he was a human soul. Matthew and Nathaniel are the guides that work with me. My main spirit guide, Luke, was considered to be an intelligent writer and scholar during biblical days in human form. He has a section featured in the Bible called the Book of Luke. One of my Guardian Angels, Veronica, wiped the face of Jesus before the crucifixion according to some texts. She allegedly appeared as human to the physical eyes which is not uncommon of an angel.

My Spirit Guide, Enoch, is a Wise One who incarnated on Earth to teach about humanity. He wrote books about the sacred knowledge of creation. Enoch was a profit who walked with God in Genesis and never wavered even though some ridiculed him. He resurrected when he crossed over. His great grandson was Noah of the famous, "Noah's Ark" story. He is a descendant from Adam of the "Adam and Eve" story. I went to Bible school as a young child, but it did not have a lasting or profound effect on me. As someone with ADD and ADHD in a human body, it is challenging for me to retain information, especially memories from Childhood. Remembering the names of those listed in the Bible from that period are impossible. This is why I rely on my Spirit team to filter in the information naturally. My eyes narrowed with skepticism and soon evaporated as they pointed out that they are indeed mentioned in the book. It was only after I discovered who was around me that I noticed the irony. Leave it to me to bring in the big guns from the spirit world.

Archangel Zadkiel

Archangel Zadkiel aligns my vibration with those in the higher realms when I'm in the zone or channel. At times I cut in and out of frequency when important information or guidance is being relayed. It is Zadkiel that comes in and restores the communication line ensuring that it is crystal clear and connected. He's not someone I had originally called in to work with, but this was how he first introduced himself to me. Instantly he went into work mode whenever I moved into the channel space. He voluntarily comes in to adjust my frequency so that I hear my Spirit team clearly. This is especially beneficial when attempting to reach God or those in a higher plane. The higher I need to reach, the more he shows up to bend these etheric light cords that appear much like a telephone wire. The only difference is these are various different sparkly colored lights that bend, curve and distort depending on where my thoughts are. He is also brushing away dust, dirt and dark particles that sometimes accumulate around this wire.

Zadkiel is not around much on day-to-day communications with my Spirit team, but when I'm writing Spirit messages for a book for example, he is present through the entire process. Without my request, he shows up almost as if he wants to. This is no surprise that he keeps me connected since he works with clearing out the ear chakras. Your ear chakras are connected to your clairaudience. If I break out of the connection when vital messages are in the process of being relayed, then I will say, "Zadkiel, please connect me. Thank you." Thirty seconds to one minute later the connection is strong again. This is a common occurrence when it comes to the spiritual work. The many that are not around me regularly band together around me whenever I'm in work mode.

I remember one incident where I was taking some time off. My ego made me feel guilty as if I was slacking. My Spirit team interjected and set me straight.

"Angry with you? This is your crusade leader. You called the meeting with us before you incarnated in human form in order to contribute this information to other human souls. If they change positively due to it, then this is one more soul who can also improve the state of life on Earth. This is in order to help others and the upcoming generations of new souls who will stumble upon your teachings of the light over the centuries to come. You met with us and asked that we agree to stand by you and ensure that you stay on path to fulfill this purpose. We would assist you in the best way we can from this side. You know we can maneuver things from over here that are beyond the human scope. There is no anger. We are working with you. We are your soldiers on this side. You initiated all of this beforehand. We're here to make sure you don't lose faith or patience. One of the things you mentioned to us before you incarnated was that you knew that you may lose your way in the human body. And that you will be relying on us to ensure that you don't stray too far off. This is a joint effort my friend. It's okay to take time out and re-charge your batteries. We all understand the nature of the human body in the Earth plane grows exhausting. As strong as you are to begin with, you don't have the same strength you have when you're back home here in the other world. You're doing the best you can with what you have. Rest assured there is no anger or annoyance. We are removing this human guilt from your body. "

Afterword

As discussed in one my previous books, *Reaching for the Warrior Within*, my Spirit team had given me the first of many long disclosures of where I came from.

"You are a wise one who lives in a paradise world full of the greenest grass, tallest trees and brightest flowers. Majestic Castles and Waterfalls surround this. You are a magician and excel in magic. You have the capabilities to manifest anything you like. You have this power now. What looks like magic where you came from, is manifestation where you are now. You block your communication with us and what you can do when you lose faith and stop believing.

As a magician and great sorcerer able to manifest and create wonders in our world, you have this same gift on Earth when it comes to Earthly manifestations. The only difference is in the world you came from it happened effortlessly, whereas on Earth you have to learn to channel that energy magic appropriately child. You can do much damage to yourself and others if you direct it erroneously. Where you came from in the spirit world you are brawny and strong. You appear as if you are thirty years old in earthly years, but in reality your soul is four hundred and seventy one years old. *(This is in Earth years, since years of a Calendar do not exist in Heaven).* You are a hunter and a fierce warrior in the spirit world. You carry a bow and arrow that contains God's magic in it. When an Earth soul is unruly, you aim your arrow at their soul and you fire. This is to infuse them with love, which they may feel for a minute if not longer. They may have a revelation or get a moment of clarity. This is for the purpose of them avoiding the crime they are about to commit on themselves or another. Their ego takes over to gain control of their soul in these instances.

You agreed to have another earth life as you wanted to contribute much to the current progressing society on Earth. Now, you are remembering who you were and who you are. Therefore, you have nailed down your purpose and mission. You are to teach and remind people how to love, as all human souls need to remember that this is their divine nature. You have always done this and have always had it inside you.

You grow frustrated or angry when one is not following your wisdom or guidance. You were like this before and you are still like this. You have an ego, which is under much control in the world you came from and less tame on Earth. You are a *warrior of light* along with many of your other brothers and sisters who are offering positive contributions to humanity. Remember who you are and what you will be when your Earthly life is complete."

My Spirit team revealed the visuals of the Realm world described in the beginning of this book. The proximity of many of the Realms is relatively close to one another in the Spirit plane. Through this, I came to the realization of how some of the Realms blended in with one another, thus creating hybrid blended Realms. What is also fascinating to note is how they all work together in harmony. They have a job to do, they do it and it's never questioned. They are utterly sure of themselves and without signs of low self esteem or guilt. There is only high vibrational energy within and around them such as peace, love, joy and harmony. This is the counter opposite to how human souls in Earth life function with one another.

There is little agreement that exists in the way that most human souls connect with each other. The energy that exists in the Realm and Spirit worlds are what human souls crave, yet it eludes them due to the tampering of their ego. Instead there is a great deal of self centeredness in human souls demanding and craving constant attention and power. If they're not doing that, they're doing what they please without consequence. It's about what someone isn't doing for them and how their needs are not met. There is nothing like this evident in the Realm and the Spirit Worlds. I was able to make sense of it all by piecing together the images and audible cues given to me by Spirit. Through these minor glimpses and flashes, it is interesting to note how their natures and personalities shine through within particular evolved human souls. It's easy to detect if someone incarnated from a Realm on Earth because of this. They know they are needed for an important cause and purpose that benefits humanity in a positive way. Channel your awesome Godly gifts built in your soul's DNA towards this higher target. Do not allow your ego or the lower evolved to stop you from this work.

Available in paperback and kindle by Kevin Hunter,

"Warrior of Light:
Messages from my Guides and Angels

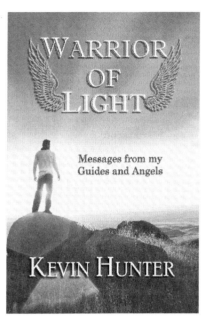

There are legions of angels, spirit guides, and departed loved ones in heaven that watch and guide you on your journey here on Earth. They are around to make your life easier and less stressful. Do you pay attention to the nudges, guidance, and messages given to you? There are many who live lives full of negativity and stress while trying to make ends meet. This can shake your faith as it leads you down paths of addictions, unhealthy life choices, and negative relationship connections. Learn how you can recognize the guidance of your own Spirit team of guides and angels around you.

Author, Kevin Hunter, relays heavenly guided messages about getting humanity, the world, and yourself into shape. He delivers the guidance passed onto him by his own Spirit team on how to fine tune your body, soul and raise your vibration. Doing this can help you gain hope and faith in your own life in order to start attracting in more abundance.

The follow up book to *"Warrior of Light: Messages from my Guides and Angels"*, is available in paperback and kindle, by Kevin Hunter

"EMPOWERING SPIRIT WISDOM

A Warrior of Light's Guide on Love, Career and the Spirit World"

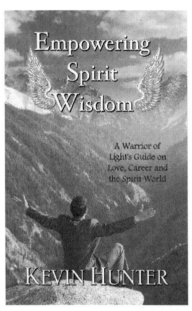

Kevin Hunter relays heavenly, guided messages for everyday life concerns with his book, *Empowering Spirit Wisdom*. Some of the topics covered are your soul, spirit and the power of the light, laws of attraction, finding meaningful work, transforming your professional and personal life, navigating through the various stages of dating and love relationships, as well as other practical affirmations and messages from the Archangels. Kevin Hunter passes on the sensible wisdom given to him by his own Spirit team in this inspirational book. *Empowering Spirit Wisdom* is part two of the Warrior of Light series of books. Part one is called, *Warrior of Light: Messages from my Guides and Angels*.

Also available in paperback and kindle by Kevin Hunter,

"Reaching for the Warrior Within"

Reaching for the Warrior Within is the author's personal story recounting a volatile childhood. This led him to a path of addictions, anxiety and overindulgence in alcohol, drugs, cigarettes and destructive relationships. As a survival mechanism, he split into many different "selves". He credits turning his life around, not by therapy, but by simultaneously paying attention to the messages he has been receiving from his Spirit team in Heaven since birth.

Kevin Hunter gains strength, healing and direction with the help of his own team of guides and angels. Living vicariously through this inspiring story will enable you to distinguish when you have been assisted on your own life path. *Reaching for the Warrior Within* attests that anyone can change if they pay attention to their own inner guidance system and take action. This can be from being a victim of child abuse, or a drug and alcohol user, to going after the jobs and relationships you want. This powerful story is for those seeking motivation to change, alter and empower their life one day at a time.

The biggest cause of turmoil and conflict in one's life is executed by the human ego. All souls have an ego. The most unruly and destructive ego exists within every human soul. When the soul enters into a physical human body, the ego immediately compresses and then swells up. It is the higher self's goal to ensure that it remains in check while living an Earthly life. The ego is what tests each soul along its journey. It is how one learns right from wrong.

The experiences and challenges that the soul has while living in this Earthly life school contribute to the soul's growth. When a soul learns lessons, it is intended and expected to grow and enhance from the experience. Yet, there are a great many souls who do not learn lessons and remain in the same spot. The ill of the bunch wreaks all kinds of havoc, destruction, judgment and heart ache in its wake. In *Darkness of Ego*, author Kevin Hunter infuses some of the guidance, messages, and wisdom he's received from his Spirit team surrounding all things ego related. The ego is one of the most damaging culprits in human life. Therefore it is essential to understand the nature of the beast in order to navigate gracefully out of it when it spins out of control. Some of the topics covered in *Darkness of Ego* are humanity's destruction, mass hysteria, karmic debt, and the power of the mind, heaven's gate, the ego's war on love and relationships, and much more.

The *Warrior of Light* series of mini-pocket books are available in paperback and E-book by Kevin Hunter called, *Spirit Guides and Angels, Soul Mates and Twin Flames, Divine Messages for Humanity, Raising Your Vibration, Connecting with the Archangels*

Also available in paperback and E-book by Kevin Hunter, *Ignite Your Inner Life Force, Awaken Your Creative Spirit* and *The Seven Deadly Sins*

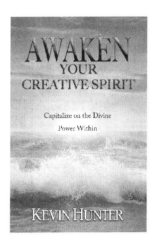

About Kevin Hunter

Kevin Hunter is an author, love expert and channeler. His books tackle a variety of genres and tend to have a strong male protagonist. The messages and themes he weaves in his work surround Spirit's own communications of love and respect which he channels and infuses into his writing and stories.

His books include the Warrior of Light series of books, *Warrior of Light: Messages from my Guides and Angels, Empowering Spirit Wisdom, Realm of the Wise One, Reaching for the Warrior Within, Darkness of Ego, Ignite Your Inner Life Force, Awaken Your Creative Spirit,* and *The Seven Deadly Sins.* He is also the author of the horror, drama, *Paint the Silence,* and the modern day erotic love story, *Jagger's Revolution.*

Before writing books and stories, Kevin started out in the entertainment business in 1996 becoming actress Michelle Pfeiffer's personal development dude for her boutique production company, Via Rosa Productions. She dissolved her company after several years and he made a move into coordinating film productions for the big studios on such films as *One Fine Day, A Thousand Acres, The Deep End of the Ocean, Crazy in Alabama, Original Sin, The Perfect Storm, Harry Potter & the Sorcerer's Stone, Dr. Dolittle 2* and *Carolina.* He considers himself a beach bum born and raised in Los Angeles, California.

For more information, www.kevin-hunter.com

NOTES

Printed in Great Britain
by Amazon